"This is an exceptional book and one of a k̲i̲n̲d̲. ̲M̲e̲n̲ ̲w̲i̲t̲h̲ ̲C̲h̲r̲i̲s̲t̲i̲a̲n̲ leadership responsibilities must read it. Too often men have allowed the issue of women using their leadership gifting and calling in the church and mission to polarize God's people. Sensitively into this arena, Mary Lederleitner provides helpful insights based on sound research. She brings us stories of dozens of women who serve the Lord in leadership roles around the world. These and Mary's analysis of them illustrate the contexts, complexities, challenges, and opportunities for women in leadership responsibilities. Mary's inquiry is well grounded and this gives her credibility to be read and heard. Her own leadership experiences and insights add to the impact of this book. Mary draws out insights that can be practically applied to a diversity of ministry contexts. Men need to read this book so that we may more effectively play our part in helping to ensure that Jesus' daughters are able to serve him in leadership roles. Let's remove the barriers that have stopped this from happening. We owe this to our sisters in Christ."
Kirk Franklin, executive director, Wycliffe Global Alliance

"As the history of the church continues to unfold, inspiring momentum is building in this decade with yet another corrective movement of God's Spirit among his beloved people. This book is a new and deeper look at our theology of women, our traditions, and our stewardship of women's experiences, gifts, suffering, and potential. In an increasingly complex and connected world, Mary Lederleitner's research helps us consider what's at stake in this shifting paradigm. From the stories of women in an impressive variety of cultural settings, she highlights the faithfulness of God and the example of Jesus, who draws his daughters toward himself rather than following cultural convention. He compels them to love and serve out of who they are, even as they navigate expectations that could press them to be less. This book brings crucially needed perspectives, thoughtful challenges, and productive language to contribute to the remarkable transformation of God's image bearers, male and female together, in this critical window of redemptive history!"
Wendy Wilson, executive director of Women's Development Track, mission adviser for development of women at Missio Nexus

"For years I have watched Mary use her gifts in missions, research, writing, and leadership. She lives the truth found in these pages. The gender discussion often devolves into arguing biblical positions. *Women in God's Mission* honors the wisdom and experience of women and men who share different understandings

of women in ministry. Personal stories from all over the world build bridges that connect what God is doing to and through women. Let's continue the conversation so men and women heal and serve together for the glory of God."
Adele Ahlberg Calhoun, author, *Spiritual Disciplines Handbook*, copastor of spiritual formation, Highrock Arlington

"Drawing on key lessons from history, the rich intercultural experiences of women across the various sectors of the global evangelical community, and her own extensive work as a mission leader with Wycliffe and other ministries, Mary Lederleitner has provided us with inviting and thoughtful reflections in *Women in God's Mission*. Sensitive to the different perspectives in churches and denominations regarding egalitarian and complementarian perspectives, Lederleitner seeks to move beyond current polarizations by sharing the stories of respected women from about thirty countries with the goal of helping women and men think deeply about leadership and service in God's mission. Calling on her readers to find their identity in God, to focus on faithfulness in service, to understand contextual challenges, and to prioritize collaborative leadership approaches, Lederleitner hopes to see the influence of a new generation— in continuity with Deborah and Esther, Priscilla and Lydia, Amy Carmichael and Corrie ten Boom, Sojourner Truth and Rosa Parks, Lottie Moon and Annie Armstrong— not only continue but expand for the generations to come. While some may wish for more extensive scriptural and theological engagement, the application questions at the conclusion of each chapter combined with the action steps in the final section of the book create abundant opportunities for readers to reflect further about these important matters. *Women in God's Mission* offers a significant contribution to the questions regarding service and leadership for the global church in the twenty-first century."
David S. Dockery, president, Trinity International University and Trinity Evangelical Divinity School

"Mary Lederleitner is a champion for Christ who dedicates her life to seeing his purposes fulfilled in the world. Now through *Women in God's Mission* she combines her own experience with that of female evangelical leaders from all over the world to inform, inspire, and empower daughters of Christ to do the same while navigating common barriers that may discourage them. *Women in God's Mission* is an invaluable guide for women in ministry, both at home and in the mission field."
Bob Creson, president and CEO of Wycliffe Bible Translators USA

"Godly, influential female leaders are stepping into key ministry roles all around the world. Their voices need to be heard. Mary Lederleitner's listening and analytical skills have resulted in a highly valuable book that provides a way for all of us—men and women alike—to learn from those she calls 'God's extraordinary daughters.' Anyone who wants to partner effectively in a global context will find fresh insights here to better understand and support worthy women leaders."

Ellen Livingood, president and director of Catalyst Services

"There are so many books on leadership, but this is unique. Dr. Mary Lederleitner has done a tremendous service to the body of Christ globally through the careful research contained in this book. She has taken a contested issue and, through her irenic and incisive style, allowed us to hear the voices of women servant leaders from around the world. I imagine that there will be many 'ah ha' moments for women readers encouraged to know they are not alone. For men, it is not always comfortable reading, but it is insightful, rich, and potentially rewarding if we are willing to listen. I finished the book more convinced than ever that leadership is plural and that we need each other, men and women, if we are to draw on all the gifts God has given for the building up of his body and the extension of his kingdom."

Paul Bendor-Samuel, executive director, Oxford Centre for Mission Studies

"A book titled *Women in God's Mission* might lead you to believe that it's written primarily to encourage women to fully utilize all their gifts in the global mission of God. If that were the only target, Mary's extensive worldwide research of women in leadership would have succeeded 100 percent. But there's so much more! If any man or woman cares about influencing the next generation, their church, their organization, or their sons and daughters to see God's purposes achieved in the world, then read this book. If you believe as I do that the *whole church* (in which more than 50 percent are women) is called to take the whole gospel to the whole world, then we need to hear and respond to the message of this book."

Paul Borthwick, author, *Western Christians in Global Mission*, senior consultant, Development Associates International

"Mary Lederleitner's compelling research relates the inspiring stories of admired female leaders in global mission from more than thirty countries, and through a breadth of perspectives highlights their remarkable responses to God's invitation to influence and serve. This highly readable book provides new insights into the Christ-centered approach of these women and arouses great respect for women leaders who encounter a unique set of expectations and pressures. With grace-filled words, a warm tone, and vulnerability, this book challenges the reader to reexamine how best to steward the gifts God gives his daughters and wisely empower them to follow Christ's call to their full potential. It is a treasure that will encourage female leaders and those who care about them in courageous pursuit of God-honoring collaborative ministry marked with excellence and resulting in significant contributions to God's mission around the globe."

Jennifer Collins, associate professor of missions, Taylor University

"In this book, Mary Lederleitner has brought together the voices and experiences of dozens of women from an array of cultural backgrounds and ministry contexts. This collection of insights provides not only encouragement and inspiration for other women God has called into leadership for the sake of his kingdom but also offers an important lens for the church—comprised of both women and men—as we seek to grow in our understanding and practice of godly leadership. *Women in God's Mission* illustrates some of the unique experiences women face in their roles as leaders. However, it is much more than a book about women in ministry. Whether as a woman in leadership, a man colaboring with women in leadership, or simply out of concern for how God prepares and uses his people, both men and women can benefit greatly from the lessons drawn out of those experiences as we each seek to live out our calling as leaders in God's redemptive work."

Evan Hunter, vice president, ScholarLeaders International

"We found this book to be compelling and carefully researched. Mary Lederleitner graciously describes the ways God's purposes in the world are furthered in significant ways when women answer his call to serve and lead. Today's churches and mission agencies must be committed to the full flourishing of both men and women to fulfill the glorious vision of God's kingdom pictured in Revelation 7:9, as all give praise and glory to the Lamb, who gave his life to make us co-heirs with Christ."

Jim Plueddemann, author of *Leading Across Cultures*, and **Carol Plueddemann,** coauthor of *Pilgrims in Progress*

WOMEN IN GOD'S MISSION

Accepting the Invitation
to Serve and Lead

Mary T. Lederleitner

IVP Books

An imprint of InterVarsity Press
Downers Grove, Illinois

InterVarsity Press
P.O. Box 1400, Downers Grove, IL 60515-1426
ivpress.com
email@ivpress.com

InterVarsity Press® is the book-publishing division of InterVarsity Christian Fellowship/USA®, a movement of students and faculty active on campus at hundreds of universities, colleges, and schools of nursing in the United States of America, and a member movement of the International Fellowship of Evangelical Students. For information about local and regional activities, visit intervarsity.org.

All Scripture quotations, unless otherwise indicated, are taken from The Holy Bible, New International Version®, NIV®. Copyright © 1973, 1978, 1984, 2011 by Biblica, Inc.™ Used by permission of Zondervan. All rights reserved worldwide. www.zondervan.com. The "NIV" and "New International Version" are trademarks registered in the United States Patent and Trademark Office by Biblica, Inc.™

While any stories in this book are true, some names and identifying information may have been changed to protect the privacy of individuals.

Cover design: Cindy Kiple
Interior design: Daniel Van Loon
Images: sihlouette: © cerenatalay / iStock / Getty Images Plus
globe illustration: © Galyna_P / iStock / Getty Images Plus

ISBN 978-0-8308-4551-4 (print)
ISBN 978-0-8308-7383-8 (digital)

Printed in the United States of America ♾

InterVarsity Press is committed to ecological stewardship and to the conservation of natural resources in all our operations. This book was printed using sustainably sourced paper.

Library of Congress Cataloging-in-Publication Data
Names: Lederleitner, Mary T., 1963- author.
Title: Women in God's mission : accepting the invitation to serve and lead /
Mary T. Lederleitner.
Description: Downers Grove : InterVarsity Press, 2018. | Includes
bibliographical references.
Identifiers: LCCN 2018028338 (print) | LCCN 2018034435 (ebook) | ISBN
9780830873838 (eBook) | ISBN 9780830845514 (pbk. : alk. paper)
Subjects: LCSH: Women in church work.
Classification: LCC BV4415 (ebook) | LCC BV4415 .L435 2018 (print) | DDC
266.0082—dc23
LC record available at https://lccn.loc.gov/2018028338

P *25 24 23 22 21 20 19 18 17 16 15 14 13 12 11 10 9 8 7 6 5 4 3 2 1*

Y *37 36 35 34 33 32 31 30 29 28 27 26 25 24 23 22 21 20 19 18*

This book is dedicated to God's amazing

daughters around the globe.

Your faithfulness inspires us to be better!

CONTENTS

I have to confess I never thought I would write a book about women in leadership. Because of the controversies about what women can or cannot do in ministry, I have always tried to avoid the topic whenever possible. My professional strategy has been to keep my head down, work extremely hard, and draw as little attention to my gender as humanly possible. I empathized with a friend's comment when I asked if I could interview her for this book. Even though she is an extraordinary leader who is deeply respected by mission leaders in her nation, when it came to this theme she said, "I usually run the other direction as fast as my little legs will carry me."

For many months God has been wooing me to write this, but I do so with a great deal of trepidation. I want to help women who are serving and leading in God's mission and not make their lives more difficult. I write with the best of intentions, but there are always unintended consequences. I hope and pray the ripple effects from this book will help and not hurt them, for sometimes even raising the gender issue can cause a harmful backlash.

My desire is to share stories of faithful and trusted women, so other agendas or issues do not derail the conversation about women in God's mission. Other people can write books that argue for their points of view. The purpose for my book is to bring the voices of respected women from approximately thirty nations to the dialogue about leadership in general, and to the dialogue about service and leadership in God's mission specifically. I learned so much from their stories and insights. I hope you will enjoy the opportunity to learn from them as well.

PART ONE

APPRECIATING THEIR STORIES

CHAPTER ONE

GOD'S AMAZING DAUGHTERS

*For me it is an adventure that I never ever dreamed or imagined
it could be. I find myself doing things that are beyond my
wildest hopes as a young mother—thirty years ago. I sometimes
pinch myself and say, "How come I get to live here in this crazy
colorful country, to share life to some degree with these amazing
people? What a gift in my life—what a blast!" I feel so very
privileged that I can cooperate with God in people's lives—and
that I can actually make some difference!*

AUDREY IS AUSTRALIAN AND WORKS IN LEADERSHIP
DEVELOPMENT IN A RESTRICTED-ACCESS NATION IN ASIA[1]

Susana is Ecuadorian, and the mission she serves and leads focuses
on multiplying communities of Christ-followers among the least
reached people groups in the world. Describing serving and leading
in God's mission she said,

> In my journey I have learned many lessons; some the hard way.
> I have made mistakes, but God has extended grace and has
> allowed me to grow through mistakes and hardships. When I
> began my leadership journey, I thought I was a tough girl. I
> thought I could do anything and conquer the world—no obstacle
> seemed too hard to overcome. I had passion and faith, so God
> and I could do anything.

I tell you, I don't think I have ever cried so much as that first year of leadership with my mission. I realized I wasn't as tough as I thought I was, or as cool. I fought many battles on my knees, and those tears in my secret place with God strengthened my soul. I also learned never to take the glory for myself because God hates a prideful heart.

Susana explained that she is still on a journey "discovering new things with God day by day, by his grace." She said, "I believe as children of God we should have a sense of destiny and seek God to know what his plans are, and be available and willing to fulfill his plans for our lives."

God's Invitations

I am amazed at how God constantly pulls many of his daughters into roles of service and leadership they never fully imagined. His invitations arrive in a variety of ways. They come during times of personal prayer and Scripture reading, or they arrive through a friend or colleague or pastor who needs help, and the person sees in us giftedness that can further God's purposes. They reach us when our hearts are breaking over something in the world that is not right. We want God to fix it, but his response is to ask us to get involved in unexpected ways.

How do you respond in these moments? Some people are bold, like Susana was as a young adult, accepting God's invitation with confidence. My response is often different. I am frequently bewildered by them. *You want me to do what? Really? Are you sure? But there are so many other people who are better qualified!* And so the dialogue goes until I take what are often anxious initial steps down a path that seems daunting or even impossible. Later, *after* I have accepted God's invitation to serve and lead, I find myself growing and developing in new ways. As time passes, the roles begin to feel normal and obvious. What was once scary for me often becomes fun. *Well of course I would do that. It makes sense. It's how I'm made.* I wonder if God laughs when he hears those thoughts in my head or comments like these coming out of my mouth. My confidence grows until the next invitation comes that stretches how I see myself, and then the pattern of self-doubt and questioning easily repeats.

My Story

I would rather focus on the stories of others, but I know some readers might want to know a little about mine. For me life started as a shy kid born into a large family that greatly valued humor. My siblings usually seemed so comfortable in a variety of settings, while I on the other hand was an anxious soul who had an uncanny knack of imagining everything that could go wrong and often thought it might. Looking back, I still wonder at God's invitation to me. Working full time in his mission is a journey filled with adventure, risk, and unfolding mystery. Decades later, I still feel like the unlikeliest of candidates for such an invitation.

I came to personal faith in Christ the summer after I graduated from high school, and once that happened God's invitations came frequently in a variety of ways.[2] They included areas such as serving and leading in campus ministries, leading young adults and singles' ministries in congregations, being a missionary accountant, traveling throughout Asia and leading finance operations for my mission organization, being a global mission researcher and missiologist, being an author, being a conference speaker (often for audiences of male executive directors of mission agencies), leading executive retreats, being a consultant on an executive team of a large global mission, teaching graduate students who were preparing to be missionaries and ministers, and the like.

The invitations never seem to stop. They involve starting new ministries, traveling to a wide variety of nations, and being willing to let God work on parts of my character so he can accomplish his will through me. I believe accepting God's invitations are essential for genuine, ongoing discipleship. The types of invitations vary from person to person, but the stretching process we encounter as we accept them shapes us in tangible and eternal ways. It is often by journeying with God down these frequently unexpected paths that we grow in our ability to trust him, and we begin to develop more fully into the people he desires us to be. And, in this process of accepting God's invitations throughout the course of our lives, his purposes in the world are furthered in significant ways.

Why Write This Book?

For both men and women it is easy to come up with reasons for not accepting God's invitations. Whether as young adults or later as we age, full schedules, insecurities, being too focused on our own goals, or caring more about pleasing others than God can make it difficult to remain attentive to God's plans and purposes for our lives. I also think there is something innate in the human psyche that likes to feel safe; yet responding to God's invitations can sometimes trigger opposite feelings. From my perspective it seems harder for women to accept God's invitations to serve and lead, for family and societal expectations often create additional gender challenges we have to navigate. For many of us, the process of accepting and living out God's invitations is more complex.

For example, a number of women mentioned the sentiment shared by Jacqueline, a North American leader. She has been involved in a variety of ministries throughout her life such as pioneering new campus ministries in closed nations and leading women's ministries, short-term missions, and church ministry overseas with her husband. She said,

> I think in many cultures, there is an understanding that there is a different way women gain credibility than men that has always been important for me to accept and acknowledge. Part of that is men are given credibility when they are given their jobs; they can always lose it, but they are given it. Women are given their job, and then they have to prove their credibility. Earning credibility for women is hard, and they can lose it very quickly.

Reflecting on her years of ministry in a variety of contexts, Megan said, "I've been told you are too young. I'm not assertive enough. I'm too assertive. You get all of these contradictory messages. You have to be in that sweet spot that is acceptable, and I don't think men have to do that. It's a tighter box for women." While these specific complexities are not something all women have to navigate, around the globe women face a wide variety of unique challenges because of their gender.

However, despite these challenges, when women accept and live into God's invitations, he uses their lives in amazing and remarkable ways. This book shares the stories of women who have accepted God's invitations, and it highlights what they are experiencing and learning on their journeys as they serve and lead. It will encourage women at different stages of their lives, and will enable men who care about them to better understand what they need, so together we might all reach our full potential. My goal in writing is to foster better understanding between men and women, so when we labor together in God's harvest fields we might be more fruitful. I agree with Carolyn Custis James when she writes, "Men *belong* in the discussion about women—not as observers or merely 'to understand women better'... but as *participants* with a vested interest in the conversation and without whom the conversation is incomplete. The full flourishing of God's sons requires and even depends on the full flourishing of his daughters."[3]

What About Theological Controversies?

In some parts of the body of Christ there is much controversy about the role of women in ministry, but in other parts it is not debated. These differences take place along theological and denominational lines and are influenced by context and culture. Many books are written to argue for specific theological or cultural positions. As I have read and reflected on many of them, the categories they establish often are quite polarizing, and frequently they do not capture the complexity of what God is doing through women in his mission around the globe.

My desire is not to argue for one theological position over another. I have chosen this approach because I deeply value the contribution of women *across* the various theological and cultural spectrums. As I have followed God in mission I have come to know women from many different nations, cultures, denominations, and churches.[4] In each context there are differing beliefs about what women can and cannot do in ministry, yet regardless of differing gender restrictions they always find ways to reach out with the love of Christ. As a result, God's purposes are furthered and individuals, communities, and the world are impacted and changed for the better. I genuinely marvel at the beauty of God's work through women who faithfully accept his invitations to serve and lead, *especially* when diverse cultures and theological streams are shaping their engagement in mission. I believe God works through their diversity to draw more people to himself, and I believe he is proud of his daughters who step out in faith so the world might come to know him.

Who Are the Women in the Research?

The women whose thoughts and stories will be shared throughout this book were born and raised in approximately thirty countries, and they have served in mission in many additional nations. They are from different generations and are serving and leading in many types of ministries. However, a significant thread holds the diverse sample together. Each woman mentioned is deeply respected by others who work with her in God's mission. Just as there are excellent male leaders, but some men are not good leaders, the same situation applies to women. I like to learn from men who are respected leaders, and I want to learn about leadership from women who are deeply respected as well. Their stories and insights should shape and inform the broader dialogue about leadership in general, and leadership in God's mission specifically.

Many books have been written about the mission of God and leadership, so the goal of this book is not to repeat that material but rather add to what has already been published. For this book I define serving and leading in God's mission as "influencing others toward

God's purposes in the world." Women in this research used the words *serve* and *lead* interchangeably, depending on their theological and cultural backgrounds. Yet each was influencing others toward God's purposes. To honor their voices, these same terms are used in this text as well. Further details about how I selected their stories and how the qualitative research was conducted is available in the appendix.

Many women around the globe qualify to be included in a book like this. However, because of time and space constraints, aside from historical examples mentioned in this chapter, the stories and insights from approximately ninety-five women form the basis for what will be shared in the following pages. There is not enough space to unpack each of their stories, although I greatly wish that was possible. Instead, when I share lengthier quotes, I try to provide more information about their context. For quotes highlighted at the beginning of each chapter, I provide a bit more information about them in the notes at the end of the book. Others I could only highlight briefly.

Many of these women shared their thoughts with incredible candor and honesty over a cup of coffee or tea, and I will do my best to try to pass along their ideas and sentiments in a similar way. I hoped to share their quotes in ways that aligned with how words are spelled in their countries; however, my publisher required that spelling align with US norms. And I always capitalize pronouns that reference God, but formatting guidelines required I use lowercase pronouns. I ask for patience as I make these accommodations for my publisher.[5]

How Are Women Serving and Leading?

What types of invitations does God extend to women in his mission? While there is no way to capture the fullness of this question in a single book, I will try to highlight some of the ways they serve and lead. What follows is a glimpse from the New Testament, from more recent mission history, and from my research with women in our current era, along with how they feel about their involvement in God's mission.

A glimpse from the New Testament. Women highlighted in the New Testament led and served in a variety of ways.[6] At times their influence was immediately evident, but sometimes their stories of obedience in difficult or unusual circumstances inspired faithful leadership in future generations. Since other books have been written about New Testament women, I will only highlight a few examples to set the stage for our discussion.

I am always awed and deeply inspired by Mary's courage in Luke 1:26–2:20. Through an angelic messenger, God shared with her such a risky ministry invitation. He asked if she would be willing to be the mother of the Savior of the world, which would mean extreme risk of personal scandal and harsh judgment by many who would never comprehend God's purposes. How did this brave young woman respond? "May your word to me be fulfilled" (Luke 1:38). Early in Christ's ministry we see him interacting in an unprecedented way with a woman from Samaria, even directly revealing to her who he was (John 4:1-42). As a result of his dialogue with her, she became the catalyst for leading a community to Christ! In Scripture we see other women leading through philanthropy and funding aspects of Christ's ministry on earth (Luke 8:2-3). Another was encouraged to take a seat at the feet of the most exceptional of all theologians, an unprecedented privilege for a woman in that era. She was offered the invitation to learn about the mysteries of God and was praised for her desire to grow and develop in this way (Luke 10:38-42).

If these things are not remarkable enough, there's more. This all-wise and all-powerful God, who could have used any number of different strategies, invited a group of women to be the first to proclaim the astounding news of Christ's resurrection. Jesus could have easily revealed himself first to Peter (John 20:6) or better yet to John, the disciple who remained faithful to Christ throughout the torment of his crucifixion (John 19:25-27). That is what leaders from that era and many Christian leaders today would expect, but God chose a different strategy. He chose to bestow this greatest of theological and missiological honors on women (Luke 24:1-10; John 20:11-18) even though legal courts in that culture marginalized their testimonies.

We also see God using Lydia's response to open a significant door for the advancement of the gospel into a new region of the world (Acts 16:14-15, 40). Paul respected Phoebe's leadership so deeply that most historians believe she was the courier of the book of Romans, meaning she was most likely the first to read and answer questions about what Paul had written to believers in that part of the world. Scripture records Paul's glowing endorsement of her character and partnership in the gospel (Romans 16:1-2). We see the gifted woman Priscilla, who traveled and taught with her husband and Paul. She was influential in pioneering the ministry in Corinth, Ephesus, and Rome (Acts 18:1-3, 18-26; Romans 16:3-4). Paul writes of his deep respect for her and says that she courageously put her life at risk for him. Paul also praises the sincere faith of Timothy's mother, Lois, and grandmother, Eunice, and acknowledges how important their influence had been in shaping Timothy for his current leadership role (2 Timothy 1:5).

A glimpse from mission history. I find the stories of these women in the New Testament so deeply encouraging and motivating, yet I also have a sense of awe when I ponder even a small sample of women from a more recent era who accepted God's invitations to serve and lead. Susanna Wesley, for example, fruitfully mothered two of the greatest missionary leaders in church history, John and Charles.[7] We occasionally hear of Catherine Booth who is described as being an amazing and fiery preacher. With her husband, William, Catherine cofounded the Salvation Army, a major evangelistic and mission movement of the era.[8] We read with wonder how Harriet Beecher Stowe used her writing gifts in *Uncle Tom's Cabin* to influence millions to join the fight and end slavery in the United States.[9] We find hope and inspiration in Harriet Tubman's story as we learn how she fearlessly helped lead the Underground Railroad. After escaping from slavery, she put her life at risk many times so others might have freedom.[10]

We marvel at how God used a woman with the significant disability of blindness to pen lyrics and hymns that convey some of the deepest theological truths: Fanny Crosby's songs are still used frequently in worship services around the globe.[11] We are amazed by Amy Carmichael, a young girl from Ireland, who sought to rescue at-risk children. She remained in India for fifty years, refusing the privilege of returning to her homeland, and her writings continue to fuel a passion for mission in future generations.[12] There is Lottie Moon, the Southern Baptist missionary who served in China, whose life and ministry have been the inspiration for exceptional levels of philanthropy for mission work around the globe.[13] We know about Corrie ten Boom, the Dutch watchmaker, who with her family helped to free many Jews during the Holocaust.[14] We remember the depth of courage Elisabeth Elliot displayed when she returned with her daughter to the tribe that killed her husband. She was filled with a tenacious desire to see them have access to the Word of God in their own language so they might know the risen Lord.[15] There is also the remarkable and humble Albanian woman Mother Teresa, who founded and led the Missionaries of Charity and ministered to "the least of these" initially in India, and then in many nations.[16]

Less well known are the "Bible women" from the Middle East, Italy, Japan, Sudan, India, Bulgaria, Korea, China, and so many other nations in the world. When Western missionaries went to new countries to spread the gospel, they frequently hired local women called "the Bible women." Their individual names have rarely been mentioned in history books, and instead are buried within newsletters and field reports in mission archives.[17] They came from every sector of society, comprising women who had once been prostitutes, women cast out of their homes for not being able to bear sons, wives of seminary students and pastors, and women from the highest echelons of society.[18] What is recorded reveals they were incredibly adept and fruitful in ministries such as evangelism, teaching, discipleship, worship, preaching, church planting, pastoral care, and medical mission.[19] As one mission historian explains, "The role of Bible women in building Christianity through the world has been one of the most remarkable aspects of world evangelism in the past century."[20]

A glimpse from our era. As we transition to discuss how women are serving and leading in our era in God's mission, the word *influence* is important because in the midst of diverse contexts and cultures many formal roles and positions are less available to women because of their gender. What follows is an attempt to capture the scope of what the women included in the research for this book have done or what they are currently doing in God's mission. These categories are displayed to show the diversity and breadth of their service and leadership. They serve as single women, as married women whose husbands do different work, or as co-leaders with their spouses. The order their ministries are portrayed is not a reflection of the value or importance of their work.

- They serve and lead in respected mission networks such as Lausanne, the World Evangelical Alliance, the WEA Mission Commission, the Global Community Health & Education Network, and in a wide variety of regional and national networks.

- They are involved in pioneering new ministries that reach college students, families, and unreached people groups.

- They facilitate macrosocial change through organizations like UNESCO and the World Health Organization to serve underresourced and marginalized people groups in a variety of countries.

- They lead by serving on boards, providing governance to a wide variety of mission agencies and ministries.

- They are in executive roles as executive directors, vice presidents, national directors, general secretaries, area directors supervising work in multiple nations, and so on. Some boldly stepped into the roles without hesitation; others felt uncomfortable accepting these invitations because of their gender until their husbands encouraged them to take the positions.

- They have first-lady roles as wives of executive directors, a platform that enables them to influence in unique and fruitful ways.

- They are parenting and foster-parenting children, teens, and young adults, and they are influencing the next generation as grandparents.

- They serve and lead as church ministry directors or pastors in areas such as children's ministry, youth ministry, young adult ministry, lay-counseling ministries, worship, educational ministries, church planting, and the like. Some are ordained and some are not, and some co-lead in church ministry with their husbands.

- They are involved in advocacy and parachurch ministries that take a variety of forms, such as advocating for Bibleless people groups, ending human trafficking, promoting life and human dignity, rehabilitating the incarcerated, and so forth.

- They are engaged in hospitality and mercy ministries focusing on aiding the displaced and vulnerable by providing housing, refugee services, language ministries, summer camps for children threatened with gun violence, and so on.

- They serve and lead through medical ministries in a variety of ways, such as being a physician to orphans, providing healthcare to the homeless, ministering to people with eating disorders, integrating health and evangelism in communities ravaged by drug cartels, and providing relief in disasters.

- They have academic ministries serving as department chairs, academic deans, vice presidents, professors, and leaders of scholarship programs to equip missionaries. They work in seminaries as well as public institutions of higher education, seeking to influence and advance God's purposes.

- They engage in media ministries with a variety of artists and writers to create films, blogs, and social media resources for evangelism.

- They facilitate the development of leaders for a wide variety of diverse ministries across the globe.

- They research and publish, stretching the boundaries of knowledge to help mission practitioners, or they extend the reach of regionally respected theological voices so others around the globe might learn from them.
- They oversee a variety of operational ministries such as IT, finance, personnel, logistical planning for global events, and the like.

How Do They Feel About Their Involvement?

When asked how they felt about leading in God's mission, the word they used most frequently was *privilege*. Many like Aesha from South Asia who work in church planting elaborated with comments such as, "Being part of something so big is incredible. The fact that God invites me to be a part of his plans and purposes is both humbling and encouraging. I find purpose in what he has called me to be and do in his kingdom." Adalie, a European, is passionate about engaging the next generation in God's mission. She explained, "There are thousands of leaders around the world who sacrifice so the world will be reached. It is us together! Each of us playing our tiny part in the big world!" While the women in this research expressed challenges they encounter as they serve and lead, they never expressed regret that they chose to follow God to serve and lead in mission. Instead, Madhuri's statement was indicative of the tone and sentiment as they reflected on their journeys: "God in his mercy has chosen me. To be active in his work is the best investment of one's life."

Recognizing Global Sensitivities

Unlike the examples from the New Testament or the stories from mission history, the ministries of many of the women mentioned in this book are still unfolding. While they are serving and leading in a variety of ways now, it is not yet clear what God might ask of them in the years ahead. They might need to get visas in sensitive locations, or they might be called to apply for positions in contexts that would normally be closed to someone with a mission background. Identifying them by name could put their lives and ministries, or those of their colleagues, at risk.

For that reason I have tried to be extremely careful in sharing their insights and stories. Most of the time I will use pseudonyms, and I will not mention their actual names unless they provided additional consent to do so and face minimal risk. If you read a troubling or sad story with the name of a person you think you know, any similarity is truly a coincidence. If there was any chance that a story had the potential to reflect poorly on any person or ministry, I exercised care and used pseudonyms because I want to honor rather than embarrass or shame men and women serving in God's mission. That is the intent of my heart because if we are careful to respect and honor one another, I believe we will be able to keep learning from one another.

Are You Ready for the Journey?

I hope the journeys of these women will inspire you to follow our risen Lord, remaining ever curious and open to how he might be calling you in the days ahead. Surely it is a remarkable privilege to be one of his children, to be given the opportunity to work with him in the world. May we too be found faithful, wholly fulfilling whatever unique callings he might have for us, that the world might see and come to know the kind and utterly spectacular God we serve!

Discussion Questions

1. Who is a woman in the Bible you admire? What about her story causes you to hold her in high esteem?

2. What in the stories of women from mission history surprises or inspires you?

3. Which areas of mission leadership do you find most interesting? Why?

4. Who are some women you know who are serving and leading in God's mission? Describe how God is using them to further his purposes in the world.

CHAPTER TWO

NAVIGATING POWER
WHEN SERVING

*Women are expected to succeed in all they do. We balance work,
marriage, children, care for extended family, community responsibilities, church, and ministry. Women receive the first blame if
their kids stray or if their husbands are not living balanced lives.*

GLADYS IS FROM A TRIBE IN KENYA AND HAS TRAINED
TRAUMA COUNSELORS TO CARE FOR PEOPLE
AFTER NATURAL DISASTERS, ACTS OF
TERRORISM, AND ETHNIC CLEANSING[1]

Kristen married her husband while he was in seminary, and she
enjoyed being a pastor's wife. She viewed ministry with him
as a partnership, and speaking of that season in her life she said, "I
was very much a co-leader." After pastoring a church for a while
they decided to go overseas where her husband took a leadership
role with a seminary. Referring to that ministry invitation, Kristen
said, "Everything seemed to just fit into place." But once they got
overseas, she said, "That is where I started to feel the alienation
between ministry and no longer being a partner in it. Now realisti-
cally, I was writing the newsletters, I was raising the funding, and
cospeaking in churches and all of that, but I was definitely a 'ministry
widow' in that position." Because the new role made it virtually

impossible to work and lead together, Kristen started to wonder, *Who am I?* She said, "So I threw myself into homeschooling the kids." For her it was a process of setting aside her power to be a co-leader in a ministry so her husband and children could flourish.

When they came back to North America, her husband continued to teach and lead in a seminary, and she found no way to meaningfully engage with his work. About this time their oldest daughter, who had Down syndrome, began timing out of social services because of her age. As a result of this need Kristen saw for her daughter and others like her, she began developing programs for adults with disabilities. After blossoming in this type of leadership role, Kristen decided to go back to university, but this time in business administration. She wanted a high enough leadership position to enable her to be involved in strategic planning and to allow her to protect programs she cared about and "staff with great hearts." After graduating she transitioned into becoming an executive director for a nonprofit that advocates for marginalized people. Now she and her husband share articles and podcasts about leadership, and she starts her day with her Bible and the *Wall Street Journal*.[2]

Is Leadership the Same Regardless of Gender?

In some ways leadership for women is the same as it is for men. Many women whose stories are shared in this book walk with others through long processes of capacity building, coaching, and development in many practical areas necessary for running fruitful and effective ministries. Women, like men, need to manage accounts, develop budgets, and raise funds for ministries. They need to work out leadership succession processes and sort out disagreements with staff and board members about issues such as vision and policy making. Melanie, whose father founded a congregation that has invested millions of dollars into supporting missions around the world, now serves as the chair of that congregation's mission committee. In her role, she explained, gender is not the challenge. Rather, it is getting the next generation of twenty- and thirty-somethings involved so the mission legacy of the congregation continues.

Women serving and leading in God's mission talked about the challenge of learning new languages, irritation when government bureaucracy hinders getting aid to hurting people, and the frustration of training short-term workers from their nations "to be quiet, listen, and not start telling people what they would do if they were in that situation." They grapple with "strengthening infrastructure, prioritizing care of employees, facilitating reconciliation," and so forth. As Brook, who leads a large medical missions agency, explained, "We all struggle with too much work, lack of finances, and colleagues who see things differently." She said whether male or female, leaders need "tougher skin, more Christlike attitudes, and a deeper prayer life and walk with God."

While these are the same leadership challenges male counterparts face, there are a variety of situations where gender significantly affects leadership. Many women's lives are a balancing act of navigating power in different spheres and roles, and this becomes most noticeable in their leadership trajectories. Over the years I've worked with many men, and they often follow a fairly linear leadership path. Economic factors can disrupt the trajectory if they get laid off because of a lack of funding, but most of the time they seem to be on a ladder, letting go of one rung to grasp the next higher level of leadership. In that process, they grow in organizational power and influence, and this might not lessen until they are near retirement. The paths for women are frequently more diverse because of the needs of loved ones and expectations their communities have about what they can and cannot do because of their gender.[3]

Unexpected Twists and Turns in Their Journeys

Because of gender expectations in a variety of cultures and settings, it is common for women to leave ministry workplaces or drastically cut back the scope of their leadership to care for young children, aging parents, and ailing relatives. While both men and women have to balance a wide range of personal and professional roles in their lives, disruption in mission leadership trajectories happens disproportionately to women.

However, the situation can work in reverse as well. In some instances family circumstances or needs within mission organizations are catalysts for women to step into new types of power tied to leadership roles they never imagined. Some willingly accept such transitions without hesitation, while others chafe at the idea. The sheer fact that they are being asked sometimes goes against all of their preconceived ideas about how they would be serving in God's mission as a woman. The following is a small sample of stories that illustrate how women let go of power in the workplace or stepped into it in new ways as they responded to unanticipated family and ministry circumstances.

I lost my only daughter. Leticia had a Catholic upbringing, and she came to Christ when she was thirty years old. At that time she became deeply involved in her church. Her beautiful daughter attended Christian school for parts of her education and grew strong in her faith. Leticia worked in business, and after her daughter went to college Leticia was supposed to begin a MBA program. That is when she received the news that caused her world to fall apart. Her only child, her beautiful godly daughter, was killed by a drunk driver. The strong businesswoman fell to pieces. She said, "The analytical side of me wanted to solve the situation. I had immense grieving loss for the rest of my life. I knew I had to seek ways to resolve it. I began diving into God's Word. The Bible became a lifeline. In my desperation, that is where God led me to experience a depth of intimacy with him. It turned out to be bittersweet because, yes, I had just experienced the biggest loss in my life, in any mother's life. While at the same time I was experiencing God's unconditional love and care for my broken heart. God was manifesting himself to me and transforming me."[4]

Leticia took a leave of absence from her job for almost a full year. In that period of utter powerlessness, God put in her heart a calling to serve in his mission. She didn't know what it meant. All she knew for sure was that the passion she had for the marketplace was gone. She tried going back to work after six months, but after a week she left because in her words "it felt futile." She said she read everything she could about heaven because she wanted to know more about where her daughter was now and what it was like. Approximately a year after the tragedy, she learned of a job opening at a Christian publishing company, and a friend told her she should apply. That is when Leticia was offered a position that started a totally new trajectory in her life. Her responsibilities were to launch a Spanish line of books, a campaign based on a book about heaven for Latin markets, as well as launching a new dynamic equivalence Bible translation in Spanish.

Her background of launching new product lines was a perfect fit for this type of ministry. She couldn't believe God's kindness, and she has gone into a variety of leadership roles in God's mission since that time. Leticia said, "Being a mother, becoming a single parent, then the unimaginable loss, followed by a clear calling to ministry work, including Bible translation ... looking back I see God's fingerprints all over, forming and molding me to serve in ministry."

I left an abusive husband. In Ellie's situation, life began unfolding in ways she had never anticipated. She was raised in a great home and always had a passion for God and his kingdom. She married young and had several children. Later, abuse erupted in her marriage, and it grew more violent as time progressed. Finally, she had no option but to leave her husband. That is when God called her to follow him and step into leadership in his mission. She explained,

> It's a nightmare [referencing the abuse she encountered in her marriage]. God does not fit any boxes. I was sitting on my bed crying to the Lord saying, "It does not make sense. I am a woman. I am going to be a divorced woman. And you are calling me to be a pastor? *What* are you doing? That will never work!" ... I had just said, "This is *insane!*" and the Lord said to me, "I have anointed you to preach the good news to the poor, to break the chains of the oppressed." Okay. Okay. But I don't understand. Really it has been a continuing yielding of my own understanding of who I am and what I can do, to what God has called me to do, and just obedience.

She enrolled in seminary, and now with her pastoral training Ellie serves as the area director of an organization that works with trafficked girls and women in the Middle East. Though she once felt powerless, God redeemed the abuse she suffered and now works through her in powerful and healing ways as she leads and walks with others through painful circumstances.

My mission asked me to lead. While some women welcome opportunities to lead in roles that come with high levels of organizational power, two women's stories highlight the struggle of other women when they were asked to lead in ways that did not fit their mental models of what they thought was appropriate for women. I share their stories so we might grow in understanding about the differing ways women experience new invitations to serve and lead in God's mission. For example, Joan is from New Zealand, and she shared a job with her husband for the first twenty years of ministry, though her primary role was homeschooling their children. She explained,

> When we returned home and left both kids at university, we returned to Africa and the mission asked me to fill a human resource director position for a regional office in the international mission we had served until that time. My husband was asked to fill a position in a national mission. Both missions were based in the same African nation. Initially I found this proposed "separation" in ministry to be personally hard, almost disrespectful. It clashed with my personal value system of being a "helpmate" to my husband. However as we talked and prayed about it, we agreed that God was leading and the mission had valid strategic reasons to ask us to serve in this way for a period of time. We both thrived and grew during this period.
>
> Two years later, as my husband continued to serve in the national organization, the international mission asked me to fill an area director position. This required me to travel across Africa periodically. Again this clashed with my concept of what it meant to be a "helpmate" to my husband. Again we talked

and prayed about it, and my husband urged me to take the position. So I filled this position for the next six years.

Joan was happy later when it was possible to again share a leadership role with her husband, and they divided the responsibilities into their different areas of giftedness. Stepping into leadership roles on her own that carried far greater power within the ministry never aligned with Joan's expectations about serving as a woman in mission, yet that was the path God was unfolding before her.

Julia is South African, and she shared a bit about her journey as well as her thoughts and feelings along the way.

In my culture, women are expected to defer to men. Women in leadership are often caricatured as henpeckers. I found myself shying away from leadership positions to avoid being viewed this way. Once I was asked to take a leadership position, but I declined because structurally it would have put me above my husband at the time. Later, when my husband was appointed as a national director in our mission, I felt differently about accepting a leadership role, as it would not have caused my husband to lose face.

Currently my husband and I both serve in senior leadership roles, and even now I always defer to my husband in the case of a clash of dates, for example. Some have urged me to be more assertive, but I find it is possible to reconcile our cultural and work expectations, and to balance marriage and ministry, in such a way that my work never suffers.

Admittedly, there were times when I wondered if God would ever open the door for me to serve where I felt he was tugging at my heart to lead. At times, I confess, I struggled with a sense that I was living in the shadow of my husband, who has always been in leadership. Many years passed before I had the opportunity to lead in a formal capacity. I learned in these years of waiting for God's timing that leadership is a matter of influence more than position.

Later Julia explained, "The waiting period proved to be a golden opportunity for the character of a leader to be formed in me, so that by the time I was appointed to a formal position, it was God's desire, not mine."

My husband was killed. Esther told me the story of her mother, Eun-Ae. She was from a culture where when women marry, the public focus is almost exclusively on the husband's ministry. Eun-Ae had always been traditional like that, setting aside her own desires for further education and ministry involvement to raise a family and support her husband. But when her husband was killed in an automobile accident, everything changed. He had founded a ministry that was training and mentoring leaders throughout a restricted-access nation, and it had a great reputation. Shortly after his death the board members of the ministry approached Eun-Ae and strongly exhorted her to take over as the executive director of the ministry. Esther recounted her mother's story:

> As you know, leadership in the Asian context is very much set within the high power distance.[5] But when a woman comes into that picture, there's a little bit of a different dynamic because I think a woman in most of these contexts has less power, even before you head to the planning table.
>
> But, at least with my mother's case, I saw her become a benevolent hero leader who in essence acted like the mother

figure. So, it's your mom, so you can go to her with all your honest struggles, but at the same time she is going to speak truth into your life in the most gentle way that mothers do. And yet firm! Because they were your parents, you have to listen.

So I find in her current situation these students of my father who have become renowned leaders and have a hard time having truth spoken into their lives now seem surprisingly humble and obedient before my mother's rebukes. She is the only one who can keep them in check. If someone has a problem with another brother, they generally come to her to help settle disputes. And I think it is because she doesn't come with a huge ego. That is out of the way, and they can get down into the deep things.

Esther's dad was very gifted and a ministry innovator. She said, "But at the same time, it wasn't a very sustainable model. And so, when my mom came in, she was able to exercise a different style than his where it really required more than one person to head up a ministry." Esther described how her mom blossomed from a traditional housewife into a remarkable leader who grew the ministry substantially, raised large amounts of funding, and had the ability to draw talented people to work with the organization.

My church asked me. Women I know have been asked quite un-expectedly to pastor churches after returning from many years of overseas service, and often they are surprised that congregations want them to lead in this way. In a situation in Europe, the invitation came because the denomination was struggling to find a qualified pastor who believed in the basic tenets of evangelicalism. In another, Carol and her husband had been members of the church before they went overseas. When church leaders knew they were coming back, they asked if Carol (who served previously as an elder in the church) would be their Minister of Congregational Life. She explained, "Though this position did not require ordination, the church considered and treated me as an associate pastor." In that role she led in many ways, including community outreach and helping a Hispanic congregation to find a home in their church. She said, "It was a big change for me." I first met Carol when she was in this role, and I was always deeply impressed by the quality of her leadership. Laypeople in her congregation often told me how much they valued and respected her leadership as well.[6]

Finding Their Voice and Their Way

These are some of the ways women navigate power as they serve and lead in God's mission. Across the broader spectrum, some struggle as they leave their nation, where they have great freedom and power, to instead serve in countries where women are viewed as property or as second-class citizens. In those contexts, if they are married they might have to walk behind their husbands in public, and they set aside much of their power for the trade-off of possibly reaching people with the love of Christ.

One friend arrived in a restricted-access country and had to change her entire ministry strategy. Rather than train pastors, which is what her mission sent her to do, she realized the only way she would have an impact was by working with pastors' wives who had little formal education. These pastors' wives later trained hundreds of other women, and the church in the nation grew substantially as a result. Later my friend returned to a leadership role where she mentored pastors and even presidents of theological institutions. This ability to navigate power when diverse leadership roles and opportunities arise or disappear is a fascinating feature that is often much more unique and common in women's leadership journeys.

Discussion Questions

1. What leadership challenges bring out the best in you, and which ones do you find most difficult to navigate? Please explain.

2. Have you ever encountered the leadership of a godly and deeply gifted woman? If so, what impact did her leadership have on you?

3. Is it difficult for you to set aside power for the benefit of others? Why or why not?

4. What are your thoughts and feelings when you sense God is asking you to lead in new ways, or when you find yourself in circumstances that you have not anticipated and others need you to lead?

CHAPTER THREE

BEING AUTHENTIC
WHEN LEADING

When God invites you to the table of leadership, your responsibility
is to say yes. No other response is appropriate.

MARIE IS FILIPINA AND LEADS CAMPUS MINISTRIES
IN HER NATION, AND HAS SERVED IN LEADERSHIP
IN OTHER COUNTRIES AS WELL[1]

*T*he first step to remaining authentic as a leader is saying yes when God extends an invitation for you to serve and lead. This chapter's epigraph is the sage advice Marie received from a woman who mentored her when she was a young adult, and it continues to shape her decisions. The advice is built on the premise that God alone is all-powerful and all-knowing, and only he truly understands the scope of what you are capable of doing as you follow him in mission, and what is beyond your capabilities in light of the gifts and talents he gave you. But remaining open and saying yes to God's ongoing invitations throughout our lives can be challenging because it often pulls us out of our comfort zones. However, as we accept invitations to serve and lead in new ways, we grow ever deeper and closer to him. Leena's story illustrates what this can be like.

I came into this position as director. I was quickly asked to come to international meetings. I was nominated for the board. I got the board position, and then I was made an officer on the board. You know, it's been growing. And I think for me personally it's been very clear that it is God calling me, and he is opening doors. I've been listening to God for years, way before this director role came up. "I am willing to serve you. I want to serve you, Lord, and I will say yes."

It is very clear. I go back to that often. It's about saying yes, Lord. And so I don't know what that will mean. I don't know what more lies ahead. I just know that sometimes the task can seem pretty daunting and big and scary. But I know I have said to the Lord—I have this personal agreement with him to say yes.

That's my default, really. And I want to be a person who says yes when he calls me. Even if that means sometimes I feel like I have to walk on water. It can be scary. But God is faithful, and I have this basic trust that he will be faithful. He will give me what I need to do what he asks me to take on.

Having the default position of saying yes to God is a stance I think at times goes against the knee-jerk reaction of many women. Rather than pressing into God's calling for leadership, a common tendency is to step back.[2]

Developing an Authentic Leadership Identity

After saying yes to God's invitations to serve and lead, remaining truly authentic as women leaders is fraught with significant roadblocks, but overcoming them is worth the effort. Kate began leading in mission when she was in her twenties. She is talented and deeply respected by her colleagues. She said,

> Too often, people live out their work and ministry inauthentically, often out of fear or doubt.... When we can overcome those barriers and people begin to live authentically, within themselves and with one another, the work that flows is so much more effective at representing the community that God intended us to be and at accomplishing the task needed. If I want to be all that God has called me to be, I cannot live in fear and doubt. I need to be who God has created me to be. Leading authentically means leading out of all that I am as God has made me and in all of my strengths and weaknesses as God continues to develop me.

However, Kate explained that it's hard to be authentic as a leader if others are not willing to be authentic too, because "otherwise one person's inauthenticity will force inauthenticity on the others around them."

The world needs women who are serving and leading authentically and not trying to merely act like men or model men's leadership styles. Deborah Tannen is a renowned linguist who has done extensive research on the unique challenges facing women in the workplace. She explains that images of male authority, such as those used in the military or in sports metaphors, most often shape the topic of leadership.[3] Tannen says that a woman who is a leader is "in a double bind. Everything she does to enhance her assertiveness risks undercutting her femininity, in the eyes of others. And everything she does to fit expectations of how a woman should talk risks undercutting the impression of competence."[4] She explains that because of the double bind, languages are often "rich in words to describe such unwomanly women."[5] They include uncomplimentary phrases in the workplace such as being a mother hen, mother bear, schoolmarm, cruel stepmother, dragon lady, cat woman, witch, and of course the term I especially dislike that rhymes with witch.[6] Tannen explains, "All this means that women in positions of authority face a special challenge. Our expectations for how a person in authority should behave are at odds with our expectations for how a woman should behave."[7]

Women face these challenges in many societies across the globe, yet the women whose insights are referenced in this book are respected leaders in their ministry contexts. It might be a bit easier for women leading in God's mission, in contrast to those leading in some other professions, because character qualities such as love, peace, patience, kindness, goodness, faithfulness, gentleness, and self-control are taught in Scripture as being marks of spiritual maturity (Galatians 5:22-23). Yet many still feel the social pressures their gender evokes when they step out and lead, especially when the context includes both genders.

Recognizing Seeds of Leadership in Childhood

Sometimes it helps when women look back on their lives and see they were displaying leadership tendencies even at a young age. Victoria is an especially gifted young leader who recalled a story from her childhood. Her older brother went to elementary school and was given an acrostic assignment. The word *happiness* was written vertically and beside each letter he was to list a word starting with that letter that made him happy. He listed things like horses, apples, ponies, ice cream, and so on. Four-year-old Victoria asked her mom if she could do it too. Victoria observed, "Our answers were the same everywhere except for the letter *i*. For me, happiness was being 'in charge.'" She said her mom wondered what was in store for her, but this young leader had a grandmother and a great-grandmother who were powerful preachers, so she came from a long line of strong, gifted women. Victoria noted, "I came out of the womb planning things." Charlotte from the Netherlands recognized this about herself as well: "Through the years I came to understand that some kind of leadership was in me already as a young girl."

Accepting the Mandate and Challenge

Angelika from Germany explained the path she followed trying to navigate her new identity as a leader when she became the executive director for her mission. She explained it as a four-phase "mandate." Speaking of this period in her life she reflected:

> First, God was giving me a mandate for leadership. I felt very strongly called by God. Second, that calling was strongly confirmed by my church. The whole leadership and body said, "We can really see that." Third, members in my organization also gave me a mandate. The former director said, "I'm so happy you are here."

But Angelika realized one more "mandate" was necessary. She said, "I have to give myself a mandate. I have to say I am a leader. I want to lead."

Angelika said she realized that if she had a gift of leadership and was not using it, she was insulting the Holy Spirit, who had given her these gifts. Her advice to women was, "Just enjoy being a leader, and do not excuse yourself. That is so important! Because in the beginning I was asked, 'Are you the director?' And I used to laugh and say, 'I guess so.' Or 'What are you doing with your mission agency?'

I would answer, 'I'm working in the office.' I could not say it. It was so funny. And in the end I thought, *I love leading! It's great!* In a good way, be self-assured and self-affirmed. Yeah, I am the director."[8]

Felecia is a respected African American leader, and younger African American women frequently ask her to be their mentor. She said after listening for a few sessions she often asks them, "How much time do you have to waste?" That usually takes them back, and then she says, "What you need to understand clearly is what your calling is. And how much time will it be until you step into that calling? Because that might mean you have to step away from this prestigious position to lead honestly, so that there are no strings holding you from saying what you need to say, and doing what you need to do."[9] So being authentic requires being honest about who you are and how you are made, as well as accepting the leadership mantle God is asking you to carry.

The Minority Identity Development Model

As a woman learns to navigate her identity as an authentic leader in new and growing ways, the Minority Identity Development Model can provide a window into the challenges she faces.[10] The theory first arose in the 1970s to describe how race and marginalization were impacting people within different societies. The five-stage process is not always linear, for sometimes difficulties and challenges can cause a person to retreat to earlier phases of development. However, many who have been minorities in the workplace, because of their gender or race or other reasons, can often identify with the process. I will illustrate the theory in light of gender issues that arise for women leading in different parts of the world.

The first stage is conforming to male leadership patterns. A woman in this phase leads like a man because she believes "men are better leaders" innately because of their gender. Nicole is Kenyan, and she said in her country there is a phrase for these women: "men in skirts." Outwardly they might look like a woman, but all of their leadership actions are like a man.

The second phase is dissonance or confusion, where women begin to feel frustrated that significant parts of who they are should not have to remain hidden. Ruth, a First Nations leader involved in church planting and Bible translation, made a comment that revealed she might be in this place. Growing up she deeply respected her dad, but she saw her mom as weak. She also saw women as vulnerable to sexual assault, so she started dressing, behaving, and leading like a man. She said, "So I've seen I have to work on this side of me, to be sensitive that I need to be more like myself as a woman and not keep acting as a man."

The third phase is resistance, the idea that there is nothing positive about male leadership. None of the women in my research seemed to be in this phase. However, it can be seen in many societies around the world. It is perhaps the ugliest side of feminist movements when women get trapped in the place of male bashing, viewing men as inferior, and thinking women are always smarter or better leaders.

The fourth phase is introspection, a place of selective trust and distrust of themselves and the contribution of both genders. Nydia is a Latina and the first female area director for her mission leading the work in the Western hemisphere. Her comments capture this stage well:

> Raising boys, I've learned to appreciate how boys and men think. I don't see men or male leaders in a negative way. They have a way of thinking that is different than mine. . . . If I'm in a more dominant male setting, I have to adapt to that way of thinking if I want to be heard. You have to talk the way they do to be

heard. I don't see it as bad changing back and forth. I'm not all the time here or there. Knowing how to do that back and forth is the challenge. Sometimes I'm so much in the thinking, I forget how much I need a feeling type of conversation.

For example I appreciate that male thinking focuses on one thing. My tendency is to go all over the place. I really appreciate that. However, I can feel I wish I was like them. Then I feel I'm not adequate because I can't be like them. But I'm learning to appreciate the things I can do that they can't, and they see that. They see it. Others have to realize there is male and female, and there are things they will never be able to do.

The last phase is the synergistic stage. It is a place where a woman has confidence in her values and approach to leadership in a mixed-gender workplace. She desires to eliminate oppression and barriers to people in general, including those faced by women, and her great desire is to see each person flourish to their potential. A leader like Hannah seems to reflect this phase. In her work in global strategy she sought to develop and implement a model of collaboration that now makes it far easier for people from diverse cultures and contexts to participate, and she is passionate about mentoring and helping people regardless of gender.

Remaining Authentic in Intercultural Ministry

Several women mentioned the importance of remaining authentic when serving and leading. Yet mission by nature often requires that we adapt our styles as a sign of love and care for others, and doing so is usually a precursor for ministry fruitfulness. After living and serving in a variety of countries and cultures, Marie said:

I think the basic "you" or the basic "me" is there. So the way I would lead here, for example, in my country the basic "me" is there. But as you go from one context or culture to another you have to change some of it. It just depends on the context. So, in Central Asia it is very male dominated. They are always surprised seeing a woman leading, so you have to really go with the context.

Jiang-Li is a young leader doing amazing ministry in a media field typically dominated by men. She said,

I think as women in leadership we do walk a fine line between having to sometimes fit the stereotypes to be able to work with people and also having to pick the times to ignore them. Because the stereotype in many of these cultures is that women don't lead! But things like modesty, dress, the way we walk, body language, and approach can definitely impact how much you are accepted. So I think we have to be very conscious about how we position ourselves.

Not Losing Your Personality as You Lead

Havilah leads in a theological context in South Asia. She has a PhD and is a respected Old Testament scholar.[11] She explained that when she has been in teaching and writing roles she has been able to be herself. But when she moved into higher levels of academic leadership, she said, "I found myself becoming 'male' in the way I thought and behaved. I identified that after a year or so. I found myself not being 'me' in the way I made my decisions." The difference actually manifested when she took Myers-Briggs tests, changing from what had always been a strong F (feeling) to registering as a T (thinking).[12] She said,

I wondered if it was because I was starting to mimic my male colleagues. You know how it was said that Margaret Thatcher was the only man in her cabinet? It's as if leadership almost requires you to be male. If you are female you tend to take on male ways of thinking and doing things. I had to sit back and assess myself and probe a bit. So now I'm trying very hard to retain being the female "me." Although we don't like to talk stereotypes, there are some distinctive components to women. And I think as we rise higher in leadership we have to guard against losing these.

Havilah said, "I lost a little bit of 'heart,' and gained 'head' in its place. And that is where I felt the balance was needed. Now I do it more consciously. As long as I'm doing it with awareness, I don't mind." She felt she had lost the personal side of who she was, and she was now caring disproportionately more about systems and about the institution. She said, "I make myself remember that I can care for both the individual and the institution, and I make sure there is a balance. That's me. That's really me now."

Nellie is French, and she talked about navigating authenticity when she became the executive director of her mission. She explained, "At the beginning, I had the tendency to measure my success in leadership in comparison with men. I felt inappropriate, and my self-esteem became lower and lower. Others also measured my leadership style with the male leaders, . . . and I had the feeling that I was not as good as men." Nellie continued, "At the beginning of my leadership in France, I tried to please people and to lead as they expected a man to lead, not showing my weaknesses, my emotions. . . . I tried to be as available as a male leader (with a wife who will take care of the house, children, etc.). Very soon, I realized that I would not succeed because it was not me." Over time Nellie adapted her style and her schedule to match who she was and family responsibilities she had to manage. Now she says, "I don't try to justify myself, who I am. I don't try to justify why I am leading the way I lead. I don't try to justify my agenda (taking care of my daughter, family). I am more confident now because I know who I am."

Being Marked in the Workplace

Some of the women spoke of the challenge of finding how to integrate their personal style of clothing, shoes, and accessories as leaders, especially when they work closely with men. I myself have found this to be difficult, largely because fashion and accessorizing have never been my strength. I find at times I envy the situation men experience in the workplace because often they do not have to navigate so many variables when they decide how to dress for ministry events.

Deborah Tannen speaks of how women are "marked" in all kinds of different ways (for example, how we wear our hair, how we use or do not use makeup, the clothes we wear, which buttons we use, the shoes we wear, the surnames we use, and so forth). Men frequently have the option to choose a style that will not attract attention or subject them to any particular interpretation, but she explains that often a woman cannot, for "whatever a woman wears, whatever she calls herself, however she talks, will be fodder for interpretation about her character and competence."[13] I was surprised when an especially gifted leader told me that she agonizes over what clothes and jewelry to wear. To me she always looks so fashionable and put together. But because she works with many men, she worries that being authentic with her style might send a nonverbal message that she is flirting.

Finding Our Ultimate Identity in God

Because of the double bind and complexities that women leaders face as they seek to be authentic in their leadership, an article in the *Harvard Business Review* stated, "Gender bias can make these transitions more challenging for women, and focusing exclusively on acquiring new skills isn't sufficient; the learning must be accompanied by a growing sense of identity as a leader." They argue that's why "safe spaces for leadership identity development and encouraging women to anchor their leadership in purpose will get better results than the paths most organizations currently pursue."[14] The only piece that I believe is different for women who lead in God's mission is a deeper identity than purpose will be needed to enable women to navigate the challenges they will face personally and professionally. Their identity must be rooted first in God, and not merely his purposes.

Neide, a Brazilian leader, said, "I need to decide and make time to adore God. It makes no difference the difficulties I am having at work. He has to be the first in my life."[15] For her, all leadership challenges are manageable if she maintains a healthy and vibrant relationship with God. Allison, who is involved in leadership development with women in the Muslim world, mentioned this as well, for she was finding women becoming so focused and involved in ministry needs they were not taking time to rest in God and find renewal and strength in him first.

It was beautiful to hear the responses of respected Latina leaders when I asked them to share how they sense God sees them and what he has spoken to their hearts about their true identity in Christ. Some of their comments were: "I've chosen you, do not be afraid." "You can make it." "I'm with you." "You are very precious to me." "I have sent you." "You are created for a purpose." "You are created to reflect an aspect of me." "I am the Creator, and I am perfect in what I make." "I've created you to be who you are, and I am pleased with who I created you to be."

The administrator who arranged all the logistics for the retreat said women need to "be led by God without fears, without feeling second class, as though we are missing something, knowing he is happy and aware of our gender and the way we are." Ana from El Salvador said,

> God uses us like he uses men. Sometimes I forget that I have an identity in him, and the way of leadership does not need to be like a man or the same as another women. It needs to be how God has made me: the talents, the abilities, even with my weaknesses and my strengths and my own personality. This is something I have to remember all the time. I can admire another woman in leadership, but I don't have to be like her. Maybe we can complement each other, but the Lord is going to use me for how I am.[16]

Discussion Questions

1. Do you find it easy to say yes to God's invitations to serve and lead? Why or why not?

2. What phrases do you hear spoken in your culture about women who lead? How might women feel when these phrases are used to describe them?

3. What does authentic leadership look like for you?

4. What makes it easy for you to be authentic in your workplace, and what makes it difficult?

PART TWO

....

THE FAITHFUL
CONNECTED
LEADER

CHAPTER FOUR

A DISTINCTIVE
FOUNDATION

If you feel that God is calling you into ministry, it is not about
you. It's all about him. And if he calls you, he will equip you.

ABENI IS NIGERIAN, AND SHE SUPPORTS AND ADVISES
WOMEN INVOLVED IN CHURCH PLANTING
INITIATIVES AROUND THE GLOBE[1]

*I*had the pleasure of meeting Maggie Gobran twenty years ago,
but now throughout the world she is affectionately known as
"Mama Maggie." I was in my early thirties and just starting to work
full time in missions. My church was commissioning me as part of
their yearly global mission festival, a time when many of their mission
partners from around the world return to share ministry stories with
the congregation.

I was taken by Mama Maggie's story; here was a woman who
came from a wealthy, influential family in Egypt. She had an extensive
education and taught at the leading university in her nation. Yet she
left all the prestige to serve among the most vulnerable, large
communities of adults and children who lived in Cairo's garbage
dumps. Daily these people scour through rubbish to find things they
might sell for money. Child abuse in many horrific forms is
commonplace, as is a sense of hopelessness and despair.

Yet, in the midst of interacting with such suffering, this remarkable woman almost seemed to glow with the presence of Christ. She reminded me of what Moses must have looked like when his face shined with the glory of God (Exodus 34:29-30). Years later Mama Maggie came to the mission festival and spoke about her work. By now she had transformed further, putting aside her stylish and fashionable clothes to wear a simple white skirt and blouse. She wanted people to see Jesus and nothing else in her work. As she spoke, Joseph, a normally stoic man, cried throughout the sermon. I had never seen him respond like this in all the years I had known him. Another large and formidable man had the same response, and so did many other men in the congregation. Mama Maggie spoke so softly it was at times hard to hear what she was saying. When I asked Joseph why he cried, he said God was touching his heart in a way he had never before experienced, and he couldn't stop. Mama Maggie has since been nominated on a few different occasions for the Nobel Peace Prize.[2]

The Faithful Connected Leader

It was interesting watching a model of leadership emerge from such ethnically diverse women who were serving in so many different types of ministries. While the women often called themselves "servant leaders," the pattern that emerged from their comments is far more nuanced. It reveals shades of other types of models commonly discussed in leadership literature, yet these only capture small slices of what the women expressed.[3] For example, at times it reflected shades of Jim Collins's Level 5 leader, whose predominant traits include humility and a focused passion for impact.[4] However, most of the women would not be comfortable with the metaphor Collins uses about "getting the right people on and off a bus," because such a metaphor does not honor the complexities and interconnectivity prevalent in human lives or the trauma that occurs when a person is removed from a team or ministry.

Because of the distinctiveness of the pattern that emerged from the women's comments, I believe a new model is warranted to illustrate the breadth and wonder of how many of them are leading. Just as women identify with leadership models that men create and name through their research, so too I believe many men laboring in God's mission will resonate with this model that emerges from the comments of so many talented women leaders across the globe.

Why They Use the Default Phrase "Servant Leader"

The rhetoric Christ-followers use most frequently to describe themselves is "servant leader." It is less a reference to the formal theory developed by Robert Greenleaf[5] than a natural outgrowth of Jesus' teaching about leadership with his disciples found in Matthew 20:20-28:

> Then the mother of Zebedee's sons came to Jesus with her sons and, kneeling down, asked a favor of him.
>
> "What is it you want?" he asked.
>
> She said, "Grant that one of these two sons of mine may sit at your right and the other at your left in your kingdom."
>
> "You don't know what you are asking," Jesus said to them. "Can you drink the cup I am going to drink?"
>
> "We can," they answered.
>
> Jesus said to them, "You will indeed drink from my cup, but to sit at my right or left is not for me to grant. These places belong to those for whom they have been prepared by my Father."

When the ten heard about this, they were indignant with the two brothers. Jesus called them together and said, "You know that the rulers of the Gentiles lord it over them, and their high officials exercise authority over them. Not so with you. Instead, whoever wants to become great among you must be your servant, and whoever wants to be first must be your slave—just as the Son of Man did not come to be served, but to serve, and to give his life as a ransom for many."

So familiar are the words of Christ in this passage that it would be an oxymoron for Jesus-followers to say they are not a servant leader.

The Seven Traits

While women in this research regularly stated that they were "servant leaders," or that they deeply value and try to live out "servant leadership," the pattern that emerges from the breadth of their comments is far more distinct. As I wrestled with how to capture the complexity of the model in a concise way, the two words that stood out most in the data were *faithful* and *connected*. I think these words capture the essence of how many of them lead. They are first and foremost seeking to be faithful to their God. Some might ask, "Who is their God?" He is the God described in the Apostles' and Nicene Creeds, though I think they would most likely also specify that he is a kind, loving, and just God, even though religious leaders throughout history have not always modeled well those aspects of his character and nature.

They seek first and foremost to be faithful to him in what they do, the goals they undertake, their commitment to follow him in forgiving others and redeeming difficult situations, the care they display in assessing whether his will is being accomplished, and their commitment to their own growth personally and professionally. However, they have an ongoing sense that they must remain deeply connected at three levels: to their God, to the people they meet through their ministries, and to the realities present within their ministry contexts. Therefore, The Faithful Connected Leader displays the following seven distinct traits. (Women who are uncomfortable using the term *leader* could also refer to this as The Faithful Connected Servant.)

1. A foundational belief they hold is that leadership is not about them but about God and obeying him. They therefore hold a different view of power because of this foundational premise.

2. They have a deep commitment to prayer because knowing God personally is more important to them than the work. They also pray to be transformed, to discern God's will, and because they know only he can bring about genuine and lasting fruit.

3. They prefer collaborative leadership, valuing the opportunity to work closely with others.

4. They embrace a holistic view of mission, recognizing that a variety of factors help or impede God's purposes from being accomplished.

5. They persevere wisely despite difficulties and injustice. For women, injustice often manifests as gender discrimination, but for both men and women, this type of leader is able to bounce back and forgive and redeem situations that are unfair or unjust.

6. They care intensely about ministry impact and monitor it regularly. They are greatly concerned about impact at both an

organizational or project level as well as at the personal level, for they want to know what is helping and impeding ministry.

7. They also model a commitment to excellence in their professions, and to being intentional about their ongoing personal growth and development.

While not all of the women in my study would fall within this sevenfold pattern, these were the predominant leadership themes that arose in the data. Many of the women I do not know well enough to assess if they embody each of the seven traits. However, as I analyzed the data I was struck by how many encompassed all of them.

Unpacking the Model

When I started this journey to study deeply respected women who were leading in God's mission, I was not sure what I would find. I am personally surrounded by strong messages in my own culture that say we have to be extremely ambitious, we have to make our own way, we have to be competitive and a bit shrewd and manipulative in the pursuit of our goals. And it is always best to keep our own interests front and center if we hope to get ahead. I frequently see similar values playing out in other nations as well, although the focus might change from being personal gain to benefitting *my* people, *my* tribe, or *my* group. Much of the world appears to use a Darwinian model of success, essentially espousing that the strongest and most self-focused individuals or groups will win in the end.

The world seems to be clamoring for power, searching for success and significance through leadership roles that will benefit us or those closest to us. Because leadership is often used as the vehicle or pathway for these types of attitudes and aspirations, I was not sure what I would unearth as I interviewed and surveyed diverse women leaders. However, I was pleasantly surprised by what I discovered, and I believe their comments are a prophetic call to return to what is truly important.

It's Not About Me

In a world that seems to becoming ever more narcissistic, it was refreshing to see highly competent, gifted, fruitful women leaders saying repeatedly, "it's not about me." The foundation of their leadership paradigm seems to be the exact opposite of the "Strong Man Leadership Model." The Strong Man Leadership paradigm is all about the leader: his personality, his wealth, his status, his power to control, and so on. But with these women I found humility and a desire to keep the focus off themselves. Here are a few of the many examples that illustrate this aspect of the model.

Speaking about her nationality, Amber said, "I'm deeply concerned with the celebrity culture in my nation—the idea that there are famous people and then the rest of us. I was being treated like a celebrity, and it was not sitting well with me." She explained that she was asked to be a keynote speaker at a large conference, and there was a sizeable team present immediately afterward to pray for people. She said,

A funnel was forming, and no one was going to the people beside me. They would only come to have me pray. And it was offensive to my brothers and sisters beside me, and it was offensive to me. So I pulled a little boy out from the front row. He was six years old. And I asked him if he loved Jesus and if he cared about people who were sick. He said yes, and I showed him how to put a little bit of oil in the shape of a cross in someone's hand. Then I put him in my place and I left.

I got in a lot of trouble. The organizers of the conference were really mad. Apparently I had the "special" anointing, and they paid for it, and I left. That's what it came down to.

While many leaders might bask in that type of attention and prestige, she thought it was contrary to God's will and purposes and wanted nothing to do with it.

Hannah, a senior vice president of a large mission, said, "I don't have a great deal of presence or self-confidence. I mean I have confidence in the Lord that he has put me in the role I'm in. But I don't have a great deal of self-confidence. So, I don't feel threatened easily—because, it's not about me." A Latina leader said, "Sometimes you really want to have your reputation. Okay, what are the other guys thinking about me?" But she said then she remembers and tells herself, *It's not about you! It's about God!*

It Is About God and His Mission

There was incredible clarity in the women's comments that it truly is God's mission. The ministries they were leading, even if they founded them personally, were not viewed as being their own. Ellen's ministry is helping many pastors and mission leaders on her continent. She commented,

When I launched the ministry, I had a clearly articulated conviction that this was not "my organization" in the sense that I did not own it; nor was I ultimately responsible for its success or failure. This was God's venture. All I was responsible for was showing up and serving as wisely and effectively as I could. The responsibility was God's, and therefore the pressure was not on my shoulders.

It is easy to subtly slip back into taking on ownership, so it requires regularly reminding myself that this ministry doesn't belong to me. Since this is a spiritual ministry, it would always be an utter failure without divine transformations. It is absurd to think that I could do it anyhow. Remembering that keeps leadership and ministry both joyful and humbling.[6]

Jessica is a young leader from North America who serves in medical ministry with homeless people in Eastern Europe. She said, "To be involved not because of my own ambitions (which we as women tend to have), not just my own desires, but make sure this is what God wants me to do for this period of my life. . . . Be humble and maintain a gentle and quiet spirit, knowing that at the end of the day it's not your work but God working through you for his glory (not yours)."

Knowing it is God's mission and his calling, and their responsibility is to obey his leading, is what gives these women confidence to step forward and to serve and lead. It keeps them humble, and it provides the strength and grace to shoulder extensive leadership responsibilities. At times in the interviews there was deep concern that when leaders begin to think a ministry is about them or that it belongs to them, everything begins to implode.

Jiang-Li, a young leader in Asia, observed,

It's the identity. It's very easy, especially if you are pioneering, for your identity to become the work. And if the work goes badly, I have seen some people crash. Their identity has been threatened when their ministry collapsed. Self-worth and everything was wrapped up into that. And I think it is just so important to remember that the ministry is God's. And so the success or failure of it is dependent on him. I'm sure we impact things, but it shouldn't be to the point that it becomes your identity.

Remembering that it is God's mission keeps these women grounded when that temptation arises, and it protects them from leadership values and attitudes that will hinder them.

Not Grasping for Power but Obedience

Whereas in many parts of the world people are grasping for power, these women seem to indicate that leadership roles were not their aim or focus. Instead, it was more about being sensitive to God's leading and being ready to step through doors when he opens them. For example, Reagan is a pediatrician involved in evangelism and community health in an extremely dangerous part of the world. She said, "My focus is not on leading but in following through as God opens opportunities for ministry." Hannah, the senior vice president mentioned earlier, said,

> I never sought leadership or even thought about it. To me it's not so much that you have to pay your dues to be a leader, it's more like you've just got to be faithful.... To think you can just step in and have voice and be a leader just because you are a woman or just because you have been around a long time, that I think is totally inappropriate.... To me it has been a call to obedience, not to a particular role.... Obedience is what it is about. If you are faithful, the Lord gives you opportunities,

whether it is leading in your community or leading in your church ministry or in a corporation or whatever. And none of it is going to be successful if you don't have the obedience in place.

Julia, a South African, said, "I recall a strong sense of God calling me to step into a somewhat empty space larger than myself. Being out of my comfort zone, I knew God was challenging me to step out in trust and obedience to follow his lead. Without this anchor and prompting, I could never have discovered the leadership that was needed 'for such a time as this.'"

A leader from Europe said, "We shouldn't worry about people who are critical of us. If [God] opens a door, I will walk through it. I know some people will not like it. I'm not going to focus on that. At the end I'm accountable to him for how I use my talents, not to the critics." Their perspective that their responsibility is to remain sensitive to God's leading and obedient to his calling is what gives them strength to overcome feelings of inadequacy, step out courageously in new areas, and overcome criticism they might encounter when others do not understand why, given their gender, they are leading in various ways.

Success Is Faithfulness

When these core values underpin a leadership paradigm, success looks different. Rather than pursuing a path of constant upward mobility, the path at times might take many unexpected turns. Women spoke about seasons when obeying God meant doing things that didn't make sense, like stepping away from organizational leadership during certain seasons to be faithful in other parts of their lives. This type of attitude is often directly opposite to how much of the world defines success. But for these women, faithfulness to the God of mission is success, even when obeying can seem counterintuitive to prevailing cultural values. They believe faithfulness is the wiser path because in the end, only God sees the whole picture.

Pondering This Starting Place

As I listened to these types of stories, I found myself pondering the profound difference it makes for men and women when this is the starting place for our service and leadership, rather than our ambitions or our desire to be known or to have power so we, or those closest to us, can reap certain rewards or benefits. Without this starting place, it is so easy to build our lives on hubris, always measuring ourselves against others, wondering if we are further ahead or behind other people we see and know. Having this different starting place, knowing it is not about me but rather about God and his purposes, brings such different outcomes. God pulls us ever forward into the unknown, to lead faithfully while trusting him in ways we never quite imagined.[7]

Early in the research I found myself wondering if their comments such as "it's not about me," but it is "about God and obeying him" were simply signs of false humility. Did they *really* believe that, or was it simply their way of coping with societal pressures in many countries and cultures that can send loud messages that it is unfeminine or ungodly when a woman wants to be a leader? As a researcher I was a skeptical until I saw this next thread of the pattern so vividly. I believe it is the natural outgrowth of their genuine conviction that it truly is not about them, but rather it is about God and accomplishing his purposes in his way.

Prayer Is a Top Priority

Throughout the research I was struck by the high priority so many of these women placed on prayer. They regularly spoke about the ongoing role it played in their personal lives. Many carved out time frequently to meet with others to pray or attend prayer retreats, even though their ministry loads were quite heavy and their schedules full. They did this regardless of the stage of life they were in and regardless of family responsibilities. They seemed to prioritize prayer for four reasons: (1) they believed their relationship with God mattered more than their work; (2) they believed prayer would transform them personally so they might become the women they needed to be so the work would not be hindered; (3) since they believed the work was truly God's, they needed to pray to discern what he wanted to be done and how he wanted it to be done; and (4) they realized only God could bring about lasting fruit.

Relationship with God matters more than the work. Emma explained how hard it was when her mission agency ended the assignment that she and her husband held in an Asian nation.

The thing I learned having to leave the mission field when I didn't want to is from the Mary and Martha story (Luke 10:38-42). God really spoke to me through it, and not in the way I normally think of that story. There is a busy woman and a woman who is relational and not so busy. But it was what Jesus said. She has chosen the better thing. This won't be taken away from her.

What I heard Jesus saying to me was that everything could be taken away. Our work can be taken away. Our family can be taken away. Our home can be taken away. Our ministry can be taken away. Our service for the Lord can be taken away. Our health can be taken away. But Jesus cannot be taken away, and he is the only thing. I was just so thankful to be shown that.

Others seemed to mirror the sentiment of a leader in Eastern Europe who said, "Remember the work we do for God does not replace fellowship with him. And it is not the reason he saved us."

Transformation to not hinder ministry. With these women there was a profound sense of their own need for transformation so they might lead as God desires and not hinder the ministry by their own flaws and shortcomings. They sense they need to have a vibrant relationship with God, but the ministries they are leading also need them to be spiritually vibrant. Speaking of a woman in ministry, an Ethiopian leader said a woman "needs to keep the soul of her leadership," and spending time with God in prayer makes that possible.

Carmen, a Chilean leader, spoke fondly of the British woman who started two campus movements on her continent. She said:

She gave me this lesson, this advice. In English it is, "I am a channel and not a source. I am not the fountain." If I lose my contact with the fount, nothing passes, so I need to be very close to God. I really need to because many, many people are asking me many things in many different ways. A daughter is asking, my husband is asking, the church, the ministry, the home—all the people are asking me things.

So I have to focus, and I need to receive my power, my strength, from the fount. So I need to be very close to God, because sometimes you only focus on the request. So you give,

give, give, give, okay. Where is the place where I receive? You need to be in contact with God every day, every moment.[8]

She explained that she had to find different ways to stay close to God in prayer at varying seasons of her life. Of this type of transformation and personal need another leader said, "If I need to change my mind and heart, then I need the Holy Spirit to do it. I need to humble myself in obedience and pray that his will be done, not mine."

Abigail, who is a self-described strong-willed African leader, also mentioned why prayer is so important in her life and ministry. She has been involved in a variety of ministries, including theological education and church planting with her husband.

> Dependence on God, this is the most important lesson for me. I have a very strong personality and I obviously tend to lead in that way. One of the aspects of my personality is that I like to control my environment. I don't like to feel that things are chaotic around me. What that means is that I do everything I can to ensure that things work out as they "should." I frequently find myself telling God what he needs to do in my life for things to work out.
>
> Obviously, as you might expect, this has led to many disappointments when my expectations have not been fulfilled. A few years ago, I finally decided that things were not working out and that I needed to let God lead the way. He has not always led me where I expected or even where I wanted (in some cases!), but I am more at peace now than I have ever been.

For her it took a while to be able to come to a place of surrender so the strength of her personality would not hinder what God was doing. She finally found that freedom in prayer.

Discern God's leading. These leaders regularly mentioned their need for discernment. Prayer was integral for them to be able to know how to respond in diverse circumstances, and how to know what God desired and what his strategy was for accomplishing his purposes. A different leader from Africa said prayer and listening to God was essential in "going through open doors." Elspeth, who is a leader from England, referred to this ongoing need by saying she is always "asking God for guidance going into conversations. Asking God to help me be wise in meetings and conversations. Issues around wanting to be in the presence of God, while doing things." Margaret trains many women serving in restricted-access nations. She observed, "The opportunities are there.... They can identify themselves as Christians. If they can be sensitive to the Holy Spirit, the opportunities are there."

A friend from Europe has led a team in "strategic prayer" to help the board of her ministry discern God's leading at important junctures in the organization's journey. Marie is from the Philippines, a nation comprising many islands. For her, "leading as a woman in the mission of God is like sailing a boat. You need to know where the direction of the wind is, and you adjust your sail so you move safely and efficiently, and get to your destination quickly. So you have to know how to adjust your sail." She said, "I think I need to really listen to what God is saying. I need to develop my ears to listen more to what God is saying and where he is leading." She talked about the need for a discipline of quietness because "there are so many noises that we listen to, even in the background." She explained,

> You cannot discern God's leading without a relationship with
> him. So I think really deepening your relationship with God

will train you to distinguish or discern his voice so that you can weed out your own voice. Sometimes we think that this is what God wants, but it is actually what we want. So we need to listen hard to what God is saying. And also get to know ourselves, so we know what our hearts are saying. So get to know God and get to know yourself, the good and the bad side, so you are aware of yourself. Really developing your relationship with God so you recognize your voice. It's like having a good friend, a best friend. You recognize the voice of your best friend.

For Marie it takes significant discipline to carve out time for prayer because she lives in a culture that can prioritize always being with people and not being alone.

Only God can produce lasting fruit. There is also a sense with these women that only God can produce lasting fruit through their ministries. Amanda volunteers her time to lead a ministry that reaches out to women who come to her nation in Asia to work as house helpers and nannies. They are from a nearby country where Islam is the primary religion, and many of the women are from people groups where the gospel has not been preached or there is no ongoing gospel presence. She said,

Prayer is an integral part of our ministry. We have a prayer time during our service, and the leaders stay back to pray with ladies who ask for prayer privately. We also have an application on our phones through which the ladies ask for prayer during the week. The ladies often ask for prayer and share thanksgiving as they see the Lord answer. We have witnessed miraculous answers to prayer. God is good!

In Amanda's ministry, God's answers to these women's prayers are the primary way women are coming to faith in Christ.

Andrea had been a senior leader in the military, but over the years she always had a passion for mission. She served as the mission chair for a couple of congregations, and after she took early retirement a senior leadership role opened up in an agency that was doing strategic ministry. She struggled with whether or not to take the role, because in the military she had explicit authority to make things happen. But as she faced this challenge, she said,

> I told the Lord there was no way I could do it unless he did the work. So, I asked God for at least fifty prayer partners if he wanted me to take the position and I had seventy in a day or two. I think I've always relied on God and prayed. It is the only way to do these spiritual jobs. There is no way we can call people and get them to do things unless God calls them.

As another leader stated, "I've had to learn through previous difficult experiences that it is vital to remain in God like a branch in order to bear any meaningful fruit." A leader from South Asia said, "I need to develop an even deeper relationship with the Lord because unless I abide in him I will not bear fruit. Unless I abide in him I can do nothing" (John 15:1-6).

Will People Encounter the Living God?

Leading in God's mission is quite different from other forms of leadership. If we are truly going to serve and lead in his mission, either through a ministry or by doing our professions under his guidance and direction, we are engaging in a spiritual work. It cannot be self-focused, not if it is truly healthy and if it is going to reflect the image of the One in whose name we are working. Prayer is vital in the leadership development process, yet for many this spiritual discipline might not come easily. However, being a prayerful leader is an aspiration and practice worthy of great focus and attention. Emma's comment captured a sentiment that many of the women expressed.

> I don't practice it perfectly. I wished I practiced it more. It is to try to keep it a spiritual work, because I can get through the day and I can get through the work on my own strength. But without that spiritual element, it is the difference between what will be burned in the end and what will remain (1 Corinthians 3:10-15). You know?
>
> Is it the chaff—my own effort? Or is it that I'm in tune with the Lord. I'm listening to the Lord in the moment. So, interactions with others could be superficial. It could be me just talking with them and me being nice and everything. Or it could be that God could show me something on a deeper level. I want it to have that spiritual element so I don't have regrets and so that he can use me more. Does that make sense?

I thought her comment made a great deal of sense. I believe it resonates with many leaders, whether women or men. There is a sense that when people encounter someone who is leading in God's mission, the experience should be qualitatively different. It should reflect the image of our loving God and bring with it an encounter with the living God. Without prayer as a focus, the chance of others experiencing our leadership in that way becomes far less likely.

Discussion Questions

1. What beliefs form the foundation for how you work and lead?

2. What aspect of the "Faithful Connected Leadership Model" most captures your attention, and why are you drawn to it?

3. What do you think about the idea that "it's not about you" but rather success is following God and obeying him?

4. What helps and hinders you in your prayer life?

CHAPTER FIVE

CONNECTED
IN DIFFERENT WAYS

We have a panoramic view. We like to take everyone in.

ANGELIKA IS GERMAN AND WAS THE FIRST WOMAN
TO SERVE AS THE EXECUTIVE DIRECTOR OF A LEADING
BIBLE TRANSLATION ORGANIZATION IN HER NATION[1]

*C*armen, a Latina, described a concept that has significantly shaped
her leadership philosophy:

I think in the new generation, well, it's different—because
I'm the older person now! But for me it was very important
to work at the same level. Because when you understand other
people are called to work in the kingdom of God, we are all
sheep. That was a very important lesson that I received from
another woman, an older woman from another country in
Latin America.

She taught me that when I was younger. And for me it was
Wow! Really! That is amazing! We are all sheep! So, whew, for
me it is a very short sentence, but it is so powerful. So when
I work with different teams, I look at all the people like my
peers who are beside me. I come and I give pastoral care to
you. But next week you can share pastoral care with me.

I think it is important. And when you do that, it's probable that you will help me when I make a mistake. You can come to me and tell me, "You are wrong in this case" or maybe "You need to pray for me." Something like that, because you are at the same level. It's not a different level.

Obviously sometimes I will disciple you because I know more things about the Bible or I'm older. But you can disciple me because the relationship is reciprocal. The only person who is upside is God. You know? Okay, you need to submit to authorities, but in the kingdom of God we are all sheep!

Carmen believes if people choose to serve and lead in this way, everyone grows in the process. She also said once she realized this as a leader, it took a big weight off her shoulders.

The Value of Collaborative Leadership

Over the years I have spent a great deal of time learning about leadership in different cultural contexts. For that reason I did not expect a great deal of similarity in how women led across national or cultural borders. Research like the GLOBE study reveals that the definition and characteristics of a good leader often vary quite a bit depending on where the leader is from (e.g., Australia, West Africa, Germany, Japan).[2] Yet, in the research I conducted, the desire for collaboration arose in many of the women's stories, even among those from cultures that would tend to not choose collaborative leadership.[3] Underneath many of their explicit statements about collaboration lay a belief that power ought to be shared with others. They tend to care about collaborative leadership for four reasons, and sometimes the reasons overlap.

They recognize their limitations. Collaborative leadership often came as a result of humility and honestly assessing themselves and realizing they did not have all the answers. Many of the women seemed comfortable speaking of their weaknesses, and that is why they actively sought collaboration. Chin-Sun is a deeply respected Korean leader who works collaboratively with mission leaders from a variety of organizations and churches. She stated,

> I could say that I have several strengths and weaknesses in my leadership. The strong points of my leadership can be that I try to do my best in order to get over my limits in my leadership journey. This should be continued until going to heaven. My confidence results from my calling as one of his people who attempts to fulfill the calling to the best of my ability. Additionally, I also try to be free and open-minded to my weaknesses. While having a strong confidence in my vocation, thus, I also acknowledge the lack of my capability.

I see openness and vulnerability expressed by women frequently, yet sometimes it surprises men or causes them to think a woman might be too weak to lead. This misunderstanding, which arises from women's readiness to talk about weaknesses, can at times cause confusion as men and women serve and lead together.

God gives different gifts. Both men and women openly choose collaboration when the focus is on differing gifts in the body of Christ, as discussed in passages like 1 Corinthians 12 and Romans 12. These passages give honor to different strengths and assume that each person will have weaknesses as well. With regard to this aspect of leadership Elspeth, who leads macrosocial-change ministries in different parts of the world, said, "To know that I am leading in community is very important to me. I'm part of the body working together." Shu-Ching, from Taiwan, said she deeply enjoys "investing in people and affirming their gifts and celebrating their lives." Many women in the research expressed joy in being able to work with others as part of God's global body.

God deeply values relationships. Angelika, who was training her replacement after twelve years of serving as executive director, wrote down all kinds of personal things that her senior team members liked, such as their favorite foods, the types of movies they enjoy, and the types of books they like to read. She wanted to pass this information on to make the transition easier on her replacement and other team members. In all my years of leadership, I have never met a male leader who paid that much attention to the personal needs and interest of team members. It is not that it doesn't happen, but I often notice women paying a great deal of attention to all kinds of little details. Because they believe God values relationships, they often take extra steps as a way of showing that they too value relationships with colleagues in the workplace.

Olivia's parents were serving in Africa when she was born, and years later she has returned to the continent to serve and lead. She said,

> In situations of conflict I want both parties to understand each other, as I believe fundamentally that if each can understand the position of the other, then there is opportunity for resolution. Similarly, if I find myself in disagreement with someone else, I want to make sure I take time to think about the issue from their point of view, and maybe we'll come to a third position that is better than each of our individual positions.

In introducing any change, I think it is important that the rationale for the change be clearly articulated so that those affected by the change can ask questions, get clarification and reassurance, and understand why it is good or necessary to change. It also means being ready to halt a proposed change if an alternative convincing rationale is put forward for why that change might not be the best way to go. To me, leadership is not about wielding power but is more about influence and persuasion and being a trustworthy person so that people come along with you.

Olivia believes leadership is about empowering others, understanding their strengths and abilities, and making decisions collaboratively so everyone can flourish in their roles.

People need to be treated with respect. It's impossible to work collaboratively if people do not feel respected. Alima from Burkina Faso explained that it is important to "listen more and talk less. In taking time to listen to people," it is possible to know others "better, learn more about their opinions and give more consideration to them." Without incorporating these types of behaviors into how she leads, Alima believes people will not feel respected. Another woman said, "Respect is a huge element in how I define leadership, and it goes both ways. I mean leadership goes with respect."

Jiang-Li is young and leading a growing and influential media ministry in Asia. Reflecting on her leadership, she said, "Sometimes there might be some subtle things. I do give a lot of deference and respect, and I watch the way I say things." Abeni from Nigeria said, "How we lead will definitely be different. What really matters is leading with respect, humility, compassion, and integrity." Karen, who works in correctional ministries, said, "You treat everybody with respect. You value them. You empower them. I think these are general leadership principles."[4]

Often, taking a collaborative approach marked by respect is what enables these women to lead so effectively in God's mission. It also helps them to better navigate tensions when a male colleague is threatened or uncomfortable with their leadership because of their gender. Jenny is deeply respected in the short-term mission movement in North America.[5] She said when she works with a man who does not believe women should lead, she invests extra time and energy. She asks questions to get his perspective and gives him the benefit of the doubt. Others mentioned going out of their way to collaborate with men like this so they feel included and respected for their contribution.

Understanding Their Prophetic Voices

What was interesting to me is something I never quite identified before the research, yet as I reflect back I have seen it with many women leaders. I have also witnessed it in myself, but I never fully recognized the trigger. So deep is the desire for collaboration and treating people with respect that when a ministry or work environment ceases to model this, a strong prophetic voice arises in them. They recognize that by speaking up they are likely irritating people, but they hold such deep convictions about how people should be treated it is almost impossible to not express their concerns.

For example Yvonne, who is an African American leader, observed,

I tend to be a relatively honest person. So I will challenge the powers that be when everyone doesn't think the same way as the leaders. I'm constantly reminding the powers that be—whether they are male or female, white, Asian, Latino—there are people in this congregation who are on this path with you. Please don't forget to include them. And often times that's an irritant because it would be so much easier to move forward without thinking about them.

Rachel from Australia said, "I don't mind when I get into that space to really challenge." She said she had recently challenged someone at a seminary for not including women scholars and female interpreters in a course that was equipping people for ministry.

Ellie also speaks of seeing women take this prophetic stance of leadership in many parts of the world as they "band together," sometimes going from village to village to confront injustices that are harming vulnerable people in their communities. She said, "But women seem to viscerally take on evil when they understand and are empowered to do so. When they get it. And they just never back down. It's a willingness to go toe-to-toe against things that are critical." She said,

It is an interesting thing. I've thought personally about it quite a bit. I have a lot of mothering characteristics. I'm still sorting out which ones are valuable and useful to me, and which ones are not. There are some that draw that strength to act on behalf of someone else. There is the clarity of thinking: "No this is not right! You should quit doing it!" That's a mothering thing.

That's what happened to the woman who started my mission organization. She saw these girls. She said, "No! This is not right! This cannot stay as it is! Something must be done!" That's the impetus of a lot of work we do. Women leading in different parts of the world see a desperate need and say we can do something about this.

She explained, "You know something about God's character. You know it to be true." And it comes out as a prophetic voice when what is happening is contrary to God's principles of love, care, and respect, and human dignity. As another leader said, "I must have harmony, but I am willing to confront to get there."

A Caveat in Hierarchical Cultures

After studying leadership in diverse cultural contexts I was intrigued to find out how women function in leadership in God's mission when they serve in hierarchical cultures. One of the women talked about her female colleagues who are from the Middle East: "The women who are in charge are always in charge." I explored this idea more closely in an interview with Georgina since she has served in a number of hierarchical countries, many of which are dangerous and difficult contexts. She has also taught intercultural studies and trained people in her field to work in diverse cultures. She commented, "You can't use the same style of leadership all the time. You have to respond to the situation you are in and the culture that you're in." In her leadership role in Europe she had 250 staff, and she led by giving people responsibility for different tasks. She explained that she handed over responsibility and power. She said to them, "How you lead is your responsibility." The key was that they delivered the necessary outcomes. She said, "We were partners together."

When she was asked by a Nobel Prize laureate to come to his nation to help change the way her profession was conducted in that part of the world, she explained that she had to take on an "old fashioned matron" or "Mother Superior" model. She said people in that culture were afraid to take responsibility because "in that culture if you make the wrong decision you could lose your job. So, their own history tells them that you don't make decisions. You wait to be told to do things, and then you do them—sometimes." She said, "So, I literally had to change my whole style of management," checking on and overseeing all kinds of minute details. If she did not follow that approach, people would think she didn't care about them. She willingly adapted her style, and she focused on developing and putting into place a lot of policies and procedures so each person knew exactly what was expected of them, and things progressed well in that nation.

Jiang-Li, the young Asian media leader, explained that her preference was to be extremely relational and collaborative. She felt that approach facilitated deeper discipleship. However, when she began leading ministry in a different Asian nation, a male mentor told her to not approach leadership that way. He said it would make employees deeply uncomfortable and would cause her to lose credibility as a leader. Since he was a trusted cultural adviser, she contextualized her leadership style based on his advice. Now that she has served in that nation for several years, she sees the wisdom of adopting a more hierarchical style, for it truly makes others feel more comfortable in their positions.

Is Collaborative Leadership Female?

Some of the women interviewed felt that leading collaboratively is easier for women than men. For example, a leader from Australia commented, "Networks are a women's way of working." Another Australian leader thought collaboration was part of a woman's DNA. However, I have worked with some men who were superb in their skills as collaborative leaders, and I have met some women who were deeply controlling and didn't seem to have any understanding about how to collaborate well. So, personally, I don't believe women are always better collaborators. But I do share the sentiment of one woman who said, "I wish that churches and ministries could work together more, with fewer divisions and more collaboration." I have the same sentiment and believe the world would be a better place if that were the case.

In addition to connecting through collaboration, these women also valued greater connections within their ministry contexts. Rather than seeing mission as only being verbal proclamation of the gospel, these female leaders were often engaged in all kinds of additional activities that addressed needs at personal, community, national and international levels. They were not arguing for a social gospel, because sharing the message of Christ's death and resurrection was essential to the message they were trying to convey. However, they believed if important connecting issues were not addressed it would circumvent people's understanding of the gospel and God's love for them. Therefore, they were not peripheral issues but central to God's mission and what they believed he wanted to see happen in the world. They also believed holistic approaches open many doors into restricted access nations and contexts that would never open otherwise. I find the research has triggered new questions that I am pondering and that I believe warrant further exploration and consideration.

Understanding Holistic Mission

Sometimes people fear that holistic mission means the loss of proclamation and the lack of care or need for personal salvation and redemption through Christ. When that piece is removed, it becomes merely a social gospel that focuses primarily on physical needs of people and societies, ignoring or negating the profound need that human beings have to be reconciled to God because of the shame and brokenness of sin. This can be a valid concern, since many churches throughout history have substituted a social gospel for a holistic message.[6]

However, I did not find this to be the trend with the women in this research. Ellie, who works with abused and trafficked girls and women, said, "Retaining the ability and the right to proclaim the gospel is everything." Margaret observed, "It is holistic. You can't divide yourself into a bunch of compartments. This is your identity. This is who you are. We see women having holistic ministry in their thinking. It's in tandem. It fulfills the Great Commandment and the Great Commission." The Great Commandment is a call to love God with all your heart and love others as yourself (Mark 12:29-31), and the Great Commission is a call to go into the entire world, preach the gospel, and make disciples (Matthew 28:18-20). She said, "I have four students here—right now—who came to Christ through their English teachers!"

Reagan, a medical missionary in a community ravaged by drug cartels, said, "We train community members in health promotion, microenterprise, women's issues, appropriate technology, or many other skills, but always combined with evangelism and discipleship." Another woman continued to practice medicine twice a week in her nation when she returned from her overseas assignment because doing so has opened opportunities to learn what people in her country are thinking, and it provides regular opportunities for her to share her faith. When patients and medical colleagues ask why she only practices medicine two afternoons a week, it becomes an open door to share the gospel and information about the ministry she leads.

With a holistic perspective, women feel they do not need to be "competing," but rather they "fill in gaps," as one woman said. Sandra, who does business-as-mission training, invests most of her time in helping new missionaries going out from African and Asian countries into difficult and unreached parts of the world. A large focus of her work is helping these new missionaries identify needs in communities where they will be living so they choose business endeavors that will not threaten or compete with existing businesses. Rather than competition, she said,

> The goal is to develop a new type of business that will stand out. We want to be a light. It's hard to be a light when we are competing. We also want a product or service that can create sustainability. A business plan is created that can pay a salary and can support a family. Then the business can be used for local outreach. The business can be used for training, for social things. It's been amazing.

Her focus is coming alongside missionaries and being a coach so they can find a holistic way to integrate their faith and ministry into their business ventures. Such integration is often seen as both acceptable and normal in many parts of the world.

In ministries reaching immigrants and people from unreached people groups, women from my research are finding creative ways to help people tangibly. Amanda helps women who come to her nation to be domestic workers and nannies. She leads a fruitful ministry that includes celebrating birthdays and holidays together, organizing fun events, bringing in dance instructors for exercise, teaching language courses, helping people learn how to manage money, learn new trades, and so on. Other women mentioned similar initiatives, and many are coming to faith in Christ through these loving, holistic ministries. Megan spoke of how she has found a holistic leadership philosophy that serves her well in all parts of life. She wants to see people grow and develop, and she can have that focus as a mom, a pastor's wife, a professor, and a grandmother. For Faithful Connected Leaders, holistic mission is intertwined with their identity as human beings who are following Jesus.

Seeing connections others miss. These women understand things like "the classroom to prison pipeline," where the number of prisons being constructed in countries like the United States are determined by test scores of young boys in elementary school.[7] They recognize the connection between literacy and spiritual development, as Alima mentioned, or the critical impact of something such as mother-tongue education on areas such as human and spiritual development, as Elspeth mentioned. They ponder gender differences. Charlotte from the Netherlands said, "It's hard to know how I would lead if I were a man! But in general I see differences. I see that in leadership women are more able to look at more than one aspect. I think they are more holistic." They believe the way they see is an asset and not a liability.

Reexamining strategy. At times over the years I've wondered if the criticism around holistic mission is driven more by economics than differing core biblical values. Often it seems to me as though the real debate centers on how to allocate very limited amounts of funding. In these discussions people wonder, *Is* [fill in the blank] *really mission?* In these dialogues, some types of ministry are valued and other are not, all based on how to allocate a part of a mission budget. I thought about this a great deal through the research, and I find myself now seeing it differently than I have in the past.

Some people might not think caring for an adult with Down syndrome is mission because that should be paid by tax dollars. That is—until their son or daughter who has Down syndrome is not growing because of the lack of resources. Another might say working with people who have eating disorders is not mission—until their daughter or sister is dying from anorexia. The same might be true of caring for people with autism spectrum disorders, at-risk children, and any number of other issues. It becomes mission for many when it affects the people they love most.

That is how God looks at people with all kinds of different needs. He sees them through his Father's heart. And Jesus looks at all of these people with the heart of an older brother who cares about his kid sister or brother who is suffering. For Amelia the importance of holistic mission became evident when she was serving in a difficult and restricted part of the world. She said, "I delivered four stillborn babies, and that was quite an ... It left an impression on me that some of these tragedies could have been prevented if they had gotten the right medical care." Attending to these health needs is mission to moms who would otherwise have to watch their children die.

It opens doors. I was stunned at the number of extremely difficult nations where many of the women had served. They often were warmly welcomed in contexts that are usually closed and extremely antagonistic toward missionaries. Because I do not want to put their ministries at risk, I will not share the names of the nations, but they are some of the most challenging places on the planet. Speaking of holistic mission one mission professor said, "The trends I see are certain areas are wide open." A different missionary observed, "When we went to [a closed country], though evangelism was not something technically you were supposed to do, you were allowed to answer questions. (And you still are, of course.) Our mission had a clear agreement with the government that we could answer questions, but we were not to take a leadership role in the church." As they lived out their professional lives with grace, love, and integrity, many people asked questions and have come to faith in Christ through the efforts of her work and so many like her.

Others make commitments to challenging parts of the world and go back year after year, dedicated to building capacity in local leaders in a variety of diverse professions. As Andrea said, "People living at the higher socioeconomic level are an unreached people group all their own. Most missionaries do not work with those groups. They tend to work among the poor, and they often don't get access to the very specialized leaders within a country. That is one of the reasons I think holistic mission is such a key way to access countries." They walk with these local leaders, sharing life and engaging in genuine and authentic relationships. These women bring "their whole selves" to their work. Their professional expertise, their personalities, and their faith are not segmented. And over time many people hear the gospel when otherwise they would have no authentic Christian witness.

A powerful example. The following is an example of why holistic mission is welcome in many nations. Georgina has been invited by government officials in restricted-access nations to institute new ways of training people in her field. Here is her story:

> I am a health worker, and I am here to provide health and care for people in need. And I do it on the basis of the values I have as a Christian. It is a holistic approach to care, and that is not quite the same as being an evangelist in a church building activity. Throughout the world we see people looking at health care through different glasses or lenses. Whatever the primary lens is shapes everything. Four of the primary lenses are a financial approach, a scientific approach, a humanistic approach, and a Christian approach.

These days a lot of people are in medicine to make money. When that is your primary approach, what is most important becomes the financial bottom line. Are you making money?

If you approach healthcare with scientific glasses, you tend to look at people as functional organisms, and health care becomes primarily about correcting those dysfunctional parts. You may see them in other ways too, but that will be your priority—the thing you have to fix, the bit of the body that is not working that you have to fix. That is what your job is.

And if you come from a humanistic perspective, you are very much about self-actualization. It's about what is important to me. It's about self-esteem, self-actualization. It's about me, okay. It spills over to that person, to help think about them. But it isn't necessarily a conduit from one to another. A humanistic approach is very much about the fulfilled individual. I am trying to get my patient to feel fulfilled and satisfied, and I'm also trying to find that for myself.

Whereas if you look at the Christian model, you're looking at a person who is valued by God. And they become the center of your whole attention, because they are precious, and they are made in the image of God. And it's not about you but it's about them. You are not coming to make money or to use patients as laboratory mice. You are there to care for them and love them and look after them. I think that's the Christian model that underpins what we do.[8]

The door for her work and expertise is open wide in countries that will rarely extend a visa for a missionary, and her work is influencing entire nations' policies and processes about how her profession is being conducted.

Two Lingering Questions

Prior to my research, I had never considered some aspects of this theme in light of gender. However, after many conversations and surveys, I now am pondering new questions.

Is holistic mission an especially good fit for women? Are women taking these roles because so many proclamation-only ministries are closed to them due to their gender? In many churches these women will never be permitted to preach, pastor, or lead a large ministry. Do women focus on holistic mission because these types of ministry doors are more frequently open to them? Semira is an Ethiopian who did her doctoral studies in the United States. She said, "In my church there in the US, I haven't seen women in the big leadership roles. I have seen women coordinating, leading, like ministry offices. Not the elders. Not the leadership. And the way I see it, honestly it's not that exciting." She went back to Ethiopia and decided to invest her time and energy in holistic mission that is now influencing leaders in a variety of nations. The scope of the needs seem to pull from these women a depth and quality of leadership they might never have found otherwise. We all know that without significant challenge, human beings tend to get bored and lose interest. I keep wondering whether God's invitation to holistic mission is his way to keep talented women leaders inspired, engaged, and growing as he reaches the world.

What role does compartmentalization play? The second question has to do with compartmentalization. My husband talks about a mental ability that enables him to compartmentalize his thinking. He speaks of having "mental boxes." If something is unpleasant or he doesn't want to think about it, he can shut it away in one of these boxes and it is totally off his radar. It rarely crosses his mind. I simply cannot do that. For me, it is psychologically impossible. I have one box, and if anything in any part of life is unresolved or troubling me, it wanders around my one mental box no matter where I am or what I'm doing. I carry every part of life with me into every other part of my life.

While I have met some women who say they are able to compartmentalize, most women I know do not. I wonder if that difference is what leads so many more women into holistic mission. Most women who serve and lead in God's mission cannot choose to not see certain unpleasant realities. We cannot put unpleasant things in a box and forget about them.

I tried to study this question in greater depth as I was doing this research, but the neuroscience regarding compartmentalization is still unfolding. As a result, it will likely be years before this question can be fully answered. While some might think it best to not raise the question if it cannot yet be answered, I think it is important to be aware of the implications of such a question as we encounter differing mission priorities when men and women work together in God's mission.

Discussion Questions

1. What type of leadership do you respect more—a collaborative or a hierarchical style? Why do you think or feel that way?

2. In your culture, what metaphors are used for good leadership?

3. How would you complete the following statement? Mission is . . .

4. What do you think has influenced you to see mission in this way?

CHAPTER SIX

PERSEVERING WITH WISDOM

If you are sure of God's leading into the position, then he will not leave you alone, though at times you will feel lonely. Various types of circumstances will make you strong and mature. You cannot wait until you get mature—your work or role will lead to maturity. If you are yoking with the Lord, nothing will be too difficult. It's very important to take the Lord's yoke and have the mind of Lord Jesus, and remember that the power behind you is greater than task ahead of you.

SANUJA IS FROM A NATION WITH A GREAT DEAL OF
RELIGIOUS PERSECUTION, AND SHE HAS SERVED
MOST RECENTLY AS COUNTRY DIRECTOR FOR
HER MISSION ORGANIZATION[1]

*E*lspeth is single and was born and raised in Britain. Over the years she has encountered many diverse challenges in ministry as she partnered with a number of large macrosocial-change organizations such as UNESCO, and has served in many nations helping to advocate for the rights and services that marginalized people need to flourish. She shared what helps her to remain resilient as she encounters challenges in her mission journey.

This thing about persevering, if I can share something my mother shared with me when I was very young, and this is partially to do with things in general, but she shared it in response to spiritual things as well. She said, "God doesn't put things in your path to trip you up. He puts things in your path in order to help you continue on the journey." So God is not like some fickle schoolmaster or someone who puts things in the path in order that we might fall. But God is there in order that he might help us continue, and continue on day by day. These challenges are not in order that we might fail, but God desires that we might move ahead in some way. Whether it is through the challenge, or around the challenge, or just confronting it.

I think we need to be careful to remember, and maybe this is just part of my life lessons I've learned at other times, but actually God loves me. And actually God is quite kind. And God isn't, well, there is a degree to which there is a testing about it, but not a testing in terms of an obstacle course. God's kindness and goodness are with me wherever I go. It's not this idea of a fickle spirit that is out to trick me. I think my belief is in a God who is with me, rather than trying to trick me.

By understanding God in this way, Elspeth is able to navigate all kinds of significant challenges and remain resilient in the midst of them.

Transformative Learning Theory

Another trait common to The Faithful Connected Leader is the ability to persevere wisely in the midst of difficulties and injustice. As Elspeth's story illustrates, the meaning-making process is at the heart of their ability to persevere. As they face hardships and difficulties in their journeys, they find ways to make meaning of what they are encountering in light of what they believe about God and his mission.

The meaning-making process is one of the most powerful tools human beings have at their disposal. It is remarkable how anyone can access and employ this skill regardless of substantial hurdles or injustices such as socioeconomic barriers, inaccessibility of crucial physical resources, limited education, and so on. The challenge is that because the psychological process happens so quickly, it can function in either helpful or harmful ways within a person without their knowledge.

Transformative Learning Theory is largely built on the meaning-making process.[2] In essence, it is how people make meaning of an issue, and not the issue itself, that determines whether something is transformative or deformative. This common scenario illustrates how it works. Imagine two women have been active in their churches throughout their lives. Both are married and have children in high school. Both just discovered that they have an aggressive form of breast cancer that has spread to their major organs, and there is little chance they will survive. The circumstances for both women are identical. However, one interprets (makes meaning of) her circumstances by viewing God as neither fair nor kind, and it is unjust that she has to endure this medical prognosis. The other understands (makes meaning of) her circumstances by believing God is kind, and therefore he is going to bring good out of this heartbreaking situation.

The first woman grows angrier, often pushing away the people in her life who love her the most. She undergoes extensive medical treatment, yet dies eighteen months later. The end of her life is filled with turmoil, stress, and harsh words. The second woman also undergoes extensive medical treatment, but she makes meaning of the circumstances differently. She believes that God is calling her to reach out to doctors, nurses, and medical staff with his love. She wonders, *Maybe in these different encounters God might use me to minister and care for them.* Eighteen months later she also dies from the disease, but in the process she seems to become even more beautiful, and in the midst of battling the disease she brings the best out of everyone around her. The challenge before both women was the same, but how they made meaning of their circumstances in light of their faith and what they believed about God made all the difference.

That is why Transformative Learning Theory is so significant. Faithful Connected Leaders exhibit an ability to make meaning in ways that help them and others to move forward in effective and fruitful ways, rather than getting stuck or going backward in their growth and development when they face challenges and difficulties. The following are examples of women who made meaning of what they were encountering in ways that helped them move forward and not become trapped by what they were experiencing.

Uprooted for husband's ministry. Jacqueline spoke of the hardship of having to uproot herself from so many people she loved. She did not want to leave, but she had to move to a different part of the country for her husband's ministry position. Someone gave her a book about actions a person can take to make a new place feel like home. After reading it for a short while, she took the book and threw it across the room because it made her so angry. All of the chapters gave what she felt were superficial pieces of advice. Nothing in the book addressed the deeper issues she was facing, such as all the losses she had encountered. She said,

> People don't want to grieve their losses. Or sometimes they do, and their whole move becomes about everything they've left,

so the present gets sabotaged by living in the past. And I said, what is that about? And I said to myself, *I have moved into a wilderness time.* And so to try to make it something aside from a wilderness is false, inauthentic, denial.

So I pictured myself in the image of being with Jesus in the wilderness. And it was early in Lent. So I thought, *Okay, I'm going to go into Lent, and I'm just going to be in the wilderness with Jesus.* And there was something about solidarity there— being tempted by the devil to give up, or using your way to take control, or letting things unfold—that made it so I could go through the transition holding a loss and present sorrow in solidarity with Jesus. So I feel like that was an important part of that move. The thing about being with Jesus in the wilderness is it's not the past. It's not making the past the biggest reality of your life. It's saying, *Okay, this is hard. This is where I am. But I will figure out what God's call and invitation are to me here.*

Jacqueline found a way to interpret her profound grief and sorrow in a way that authentically dealt with the pain and truth of the situation, but also in a way that made sense in light of her understanding of who God is and how he works in ministry. She was able to persevere and enter a new phase of ministry in which her leadership influence increased significantly.

Ordination debates in light of human suffering. Ellie was irritated because her denomination would not permit her to be ordained due to her gender. But the meaning she made of this hardship made all the difference. She explained,

There are bigger issues. And I wish more of us evangelical women would just get on with being involved in those bigger issues. I don't have time to spend begging my church to ordain me. You know? I honestly don't care about that. I think I should be ordained. I think it would be right for me to be ordained. And if it comes to a time that it's an impediment to ministry that I am not, then I will seek ordination. But come on—to spend the energy for what, myself?

What should I do? I don't know. I can speak at length and fairly eloquently about the issues in the evangelical church toward women. I truly do not think we think right about the sexes. I just don't think we do. And I heartily support women who are called to speak on that, to do action on that. But my organization falls in the spectrum of antitrafficking organizations, right?

It is humbling in an extreme way to be in the presence of these women who are our partners around the world. If our partner does not raise money or bring supplies to the babies she has agreed to sponsor, they will die. There is nobody else coming behind and bringing something. These babies do not have diapers. They don't have milk. If she does not have her camps for traumatized teenagers from the civil war in the region, nobody else is going to do this for them. They are going to stay traumatized and broken. The stakes are so high.

We are not here to have an easy life. We are here to have a life that is poured out, literally poured out, for the gospel. There is not a confusion about whose life it is. Is it my life? No, it's not my life. It's God's life. I will do whatever he calls me to do.

The ministry doors in Ellie's denomination that are still closed to women frustrate her. However, she feels it is poor stewardship to keep fighting about those closed opportunities when so many others are open that enable her to work with people in dire need who have yet to hear or understand the gospel.

The other path has greater influence. Idha is a remarkable woman. Raised in a culture that kept men and women separate, and in a church that taught that little girls were not to ask questions but were to remain silent, she later blossomed to become a deeply respected biblical scholar. She kept growing and learning, being given the opportunity to study in some of the best seminaries in the world. She later took a teaching role at a seminary, and over time she has been consistently promoted because of the excellent nature of her work, and because her colleagues deeply value her contribution. Despite her excellent exegetical skills and professional qualifications, unlike her male colleagues, she is not invited to preach in churches. Although this gender barrier could cause her to hold on to anger and bitterness, she has chosen to understand the challenge in a different way.

When I've been passed over for someone who may not have the communication skills that I have, how do I reconcile it?

I identified my gifting pretty early on in life to be writing and teaching in a classroom set up for small groups. So preaching has never been my thing. I've never been comfortable in a pulpit. So, these big extroverted things like preaching at large conventions or preaching in churches, it has never made me comfortable. I would much rather be face to face, with eye contact in small groups, classrooms, Bible study groups, or a midweek evening. This is where I'm most comfortable, where it is interactive and not one way.

If I had identified my gift to be preaching, and then I had been passed over, I would have felt a little bit ruffled over that. But since that is not something I particularly enjoy doing, I'm okay with that. And I can see very clearly among my colleagues that all this gadding about the country, preaching here and preaching there, is at the cost of their writing. I can see that happening. And then I tell myself, possibly I have the better part. That is, the writing will stand long after I am gone. That is how I have reconciled it.

Idha makes meaning of the gender limitations because she focuses on the opportunities that are open to her in areas of ministry she enjoys, and she realizes writing gives her the opportunity to reach people far beyond her immediate circle of influence.

God's Strategy of Vulnerability

I have thought long and hard over the years about God's strategy for advancing his purposes in the world, and I have to be honest, many times I've wondered what in the world he was thinking? I agree with Miroslav Volf when he says, "Christianity has vulnerability at its very heart, fragility in its expression."[3] Making sense of a wide variety of trials and social injustices is challenging. The title of the book *Not the Way It's Supposed to Be* captures the essence of how I sometimes feel.[4] Perhaps most challenging is working through heartache and disappointment when ministry leaders fall short and create additional, seemingly unnecessary obstacles and difficulties.

As I look at the situation, God's plan for his mission seems to be to form relationships with flawed individuals and invite them to serve alongside him. All the while, these people frequently fall short, making poor decisions, and at times they model behaviors that cause many in the world to question God's goodness. Yet if these flawed human beings serving and leading with God in mission keep humbly coming back to him, confessing their sins and failures, he lovingly mentors them and they begin to grow and develop in remarkable ways. Others who have to experience their failures need to regularly practice forgiving and redeeming situations, the two character qualities that most model the nature of our wonderful God. Practice makes perfect, or at least it fosters spiritual maturity if we are willing to make meaning of what we are encountering through this lens. It makes persevering in God's mission far easier if we grasp his larger strategy.

What Image Will You Bear?

What image will you choose to bear as you journey through this life? Will you choose to carry with you all the unjust experiences you encounter? It's easy to live that way because our surrounding cultures often send messages that we should bear grudges. Abigail, an African leader, explained navigating this in her journey.

Grace is the other important leadership lesson that I have learned over the years. Leading with grace has not always been easy for me. I work in a male-dominated world, in a patriarchal culture that still undervalues women. Marginalization is a reality in my world, particularly in Christian circles.

When I first started off, I felt that I had to be a better "man" than the men surrounding me. I had to work harder to prove that I could do the job. Often, I did not feel that I got the recognition I deserved even though I seemed to be doing much better than my colleagues. I was constantly fighting for this recognition, which obviously just made me bitter.

After a few years of doing this, I realized that instead of serving God in the capacity he had given me, I was trying to prove myself to men. God has taught me that I don't need to prove anything to anyone. I need only to serve him in genuineness, to use the gifts he has given me in the capacity he has given me. This has positively affected how I view those with whom I serve as well as those I serve.

Her circumstances were the same, but with a better way of making meaning of what she was encountering, Abigail was able to persevere and lead in significant ways. I believe the world needs to see the beauty of God's daughters and sons as they become better, rather than bitter, when they encounter challenges and injustices along the journey. Seeking God when we have to make meaning of those encounters, and regularly practicing forgiveness and redeeming situations, make such a significant difference in shaping the type of people and leaders we become.

Responding Wisely by Not Burning Bridges

These women were recommended by others to be part of this study because they are respected. Often that respect has been earned as colleagues watch them address a wide array of challenges with Christlikeness and wisdom. What perseverance with wisdom looks like varies significantly depending on the focus of the mission and where the women serve and lead. However, one thread in the research applied regardless of culture and ministry context. Along with the meaning-making process, these women were able to discipline their thoughts and emotions in ways that enabled them to maintain, or at least not destroy, relationships they might need in the coming months or years.

When persevering through difficulties and injustices, restraint often does not come easily. This form of wisdom usually develops over time. However, Victoria is a young leader who has matured in this way, and she expressed the process quite well.

I guess one thing that has helped me along the way is I try to trust God to open the doors that need to be open, and to be ready when that happens. There are times when things would get my ire up a bit. How could they say a woman couldn't do that? Did you notice there is not even a woman on the platform? Grrr!

I could have those moments, and I could vent those in very safe places. But I didn't let those become the things that motivated me—the things that become central—let me prove that wrong. More than anything I will just keep being faithful where I am. I want to maintain that right, gentle spirit. I have a lot of strength. I have a lot of confidence in who I am.

So I don't have to be ashamed that I'm a woman. I don't have to be ashamed of my position. But I also trust that God is going to open up some of those doors. And maybe that is too much faith and not enough action, I don't know. But it's felt like if you have the right spirit and as God opens those doors, you haven't already burned your bridges.

Sometimes if you are too strong, and if I embrace the "I am woman, hear me roar," you burn the bridges before the doors even open. And once the doors open, you can't cross. You're not trusted. So I would say part of it is just making sure you have the right heart check. What is it that God is wanting me to do and let me be faithful here.

Because others have seen her persevere with wisdom, Victoria is now in a vice president role that is normally not offered to people in her field until they are much older.

How people make meaning is integrally tied to their ability (or inability) to discipline thoughts and feelings. If the meaning-making process goes poorly, it is more natural for both men and women to think they have a right to verbally attack people or burn relational bridges. However, if the meaning-making process goes well, it usually enables a leader to understand the problem in light of the bigger picture of God's mission and purposes. From that vantage point, and in prayer and relationship with him, the truth of James 1:5 is realized—as they ask God for wisdom he provides it generously.

Discussion Questions

1. What aspects about God's character and personality do you find yourself thinking about most often and why?

2. If you are facing a current challenge, what are different ways you can interpret what is happening? Which ways of making meaning might help you, and which might cause you to not persevere?

3. What about God's strategy for doing mission surprises or intrigues you the most?

4. What are the growth areas you see in your own heart when it comes to modeling God's character and nature in the world?

CHAPTER SEVEN

PRIORITIZING IMPACT AND EXCELLENCE

In my leadership now I try to discern, "Is this going to be helpful for anything? And do you, as much as you say you want change, how poised are you to make change happen?" At this age it makes me waste less time. I hope you understand what I mean. That's my position at this point.

YVONNE IS AFRICAN AMERICAN, AND SHE HAS SERVED IN A VARIETY OF LEADERSHIP ROLES IN THE UNITED STATES FOCUSING ON ISSUES HINDERING THE DEVELOPMENT OF INDIVIDUALS AND COMMUNITIES[1]

*M*adison is an extremely talented young leader in North America who cares deeply about evangelism, yet she hit a discouraging season of life. She was motivated and creative, but her mission organization was undergoing a significant transition. The former executive director's departure caught her and others by surprise, and the board was taking a few years to find the right replacement. She observed,

> Part of it was just seeing it as a time of moving forward, even though it seemed like I was stagnant. There were a lot of days when I thought, *What am I doing? Am I making a difference?* I didn't really feel like I was.

So, it kind of took God reminding me that each of these days matters, and how do I make the most of each day? So, it was interesting during that time when we really weren't supposed to be creating things, that is when I started launching a lot of new things here, like our blog, our YouTube channel, and different things. And I started writing more because I had more time.

Speaking of her generation she said, "Younger leaders really want to make a difference, and they want to change the world, right? So maybe if you are at an interim time, you can't change the world, but what can you do?" For Madison, making an impact meant finding ways to influence others toward healthy and creative evangelism methods.

A Passion to Make a Difference

Impact can be defined in a variety of ways, and it looks different for people engaging in diverse forms of ministry. For Madison, impact was tied to evangelistic fruitfulness. For medical missionaries, impact might mean providing marginalized people with greater access to health care than they had in the past, a lessening of infant mortality rates in a region, and people experiencing God's love through compassionate medical intervention. For others, it might be the number and quality of churches being planted, or significant changes have occurred in communities because they now have access to God's Word in their own language. What impact looks like will always vary from ministry to ministry even within the same profession because it is based on a group's missional purpose, specific goals, and geographic and cultural contexts. For the women in this research, the phrase that best captures what impact means is "a desire to make a difference so God's purposes are furthered."

Concern for Impact

Some of the women listed specific numbers of people affected by their ministries. For example, Adalie is passionate about engaging the next generation in God's mission. She said, "Together we have impacted more than ten thousand young people who again have often become change makers. What a privilege to be part of this!" She also gave detailed statistics showing results of the ministry she led over the course of several years. Jane, who is a medical missionary, explained that for her "Deep down, success means that God is glorified. How can we know if God is being glorified? One way is by seeing more disciples come into being who make more disciples." Georgina, another medical missionary, told her team that extra perks such as being given institutional funds to attend conferences would be awarded to those who performed. She also noticed that some people in her prior mission field excelled while others failed in their international assignments. She cared so deeply about impact that she pursued a PhD to find answers to why some people are able to see amazing outcomes through their work while others do not.

Joyce, a Canadian, is a gifted preacher who is also in frequent demand as a conference speaker. She explained,

> In the preaching context that is external to my church, part of how I discern is anything that equips clergy I say yes to. Which is wild considering I am a woman, right? And add to that anything to do with young adults. I honestly think they will

change the world. And I say yes to every generation of young adults because that is the time in one's life when we can be most open to the Spirit's imagination and nudging. So, those are the big criteria for me.[2]

Joyce has limited time so she wants to invest it in the places where she can see the greatest impact.

Sandra is a talented mentor and coach in the field of business as mission. With years of corporate experience at some of the most respected companies in the world, her passion for God's mission drove her to make a transition so the gospel would truly reach all people. She said, "I am laser focused. I work 95 percent of the time with church planters. I work 95 percent of the time with Asians and Africans. It is specifically around business planting." She does this because these are the people who are ministering among the unreached and least reach people groups. These businesses provide an economic model so their ministries are sustainable, and having an excellent and legitimate business model provides a way for them to have greater influence in communities where they minister.

When They Don't See Impact

These women sense that they must be faithful to what God is asking them to do in his mission. Care and attention need to be paid to ensure the impact he desires is taking place. When it isn't, or when they are unsure if their ministries are effective, they start to question whether they should stay engaged or invest their time and talents elsewhere.

Lauren leads hospitality ministries that care for transitioning and furloughing missionaries. Often in these seasons of life missionaries and their families suffer loss and periods of discouragement. By serving and leading in hospitality, Lauren and her team are able to lighten their loads and ease challenging transitions. But Lauren mentioned that at times in her mission she feels "blocked." When this happens, she said, "It frustrates me. And what blocks me are systems that are not working." When systems are blocked, the people who need help never receive it, and this is unacceptable. Then she is more likely to question whether she should continue in her role.

Semira, an Ethiopian, left a prior role to join a different organization in her country. When asked why she made the change, she explained that it gave her an opportunity to be more productive because the new role provided a platform for greater impact. Annitah, another African leader, said it is discouraging and sometimes makes it hard to persevere when you are "not seeing the progress you would like." These types of comments were common throughout the interviews, and I have witnessed that for women who qualify as being Faithful Connected Leaders some of the greatest times of discouragement arise when they are not sure their lives and time are invested wisely and are making a significant impact.

In some societies there is a stereotype that men care more about results while women care about relationships. However, this is not an accurate reflection of what women in this research described. For them, *relationships are essential for significant ministry results*. Relationships do not replace results (impact). Nor do they cause women to care less about impact. *In God's mission, relational health and relational depth become part of the impact as well as a primary pathway through which God works to accomplish his purposes on earth.*

Two Additional Areas of Impact

While the women in this research cared about furthering God's purposes in the world in their various spheres of ministry, they also were deeply concerned about their impact in two additional areas. They cared about intercultural impact, and for that reason, many have spent years gaining language skills and all kinds of cultural training so they might be a blessing and not a hindrance to the work. They also cared deeply about the impact they were personally having on others' well-being as they engaged in God's mission.

Cultural impact. As a senior vice president in a large global ministry, Hannah spent years developing a multilingual communication strategy and messaging to ensure people from diverse cultures felt respected and honored. Women such as Jenny, Megan, Barbara, Victoria, Margaret, and Rachel teach intercultural studies and are careful to respond in culturally appropriate ways. Madison, the young evangelism leader, makes sure that the types of communication pieces her ministry produces are respectful of the different generations and genders that use the resources. Many others spend significant amounts of their time and focus educating and training others to respond with wisdom and sensitivity in diverse contexts. They take care to monitor and change their attitudes and strategies as needed because they want to honor the dignity of people from every tribe, tongue, and nation (Revelation 5:9-10).

Personal impact. But these women were assessing not just organizational or ministry impact. They were also regularly assessing how their actions, behaviors, and presence affected others around them. Many talked about how important it is as leaders to know their own personal triggers. For example, Leena, an executive director from a Nordic country, said,

I also try to sort through issues and see what overwhelms me. It might not be big problems, but some things trigger me emotionally in different ways than others, in a stressful way. And I try to learn to deal with that to understand myself. Why does this trigger my stress and my emotions? How can I deal with that? What is really the interpretation of that? What is it in this situation that bothers me, and so on? So I try not to neglect anything, but to look for ways to deal with it.

Jacqueline spoke of a time when the North American senior pastor she reported to said, "I don't feel your support." She said, "I would never do anything to undermine you." He responded, "I know that, but I don't feel your support." She had to wrestle with what she was doing that caused him to feel that way. She realized that because he regularly got so much praise from people, she had taken the role of trying to ask harder questions that would challenge him. But she now understood that was wrong of her to make that assumption. It was his choice to determine who would play that role in his life, not hers. She said, "So I feel like all along there is a sense of listening to what people are saying about me. Even though my first response was denial.... I needed to listen to him to figure out what I needed to do to change. I feel like there are always those types of human interactions that take thought."

A Commitment to Excellence

What works in tandem with their passion for impact is often an unyielding commitment to personal and professional development so their participation in God's mission exhibits excellence. While most people are not able to start out being excellent in their leadership roles, the drive and commitment of these women eventually enables them to arrive at that destination. This theme came out repeatedly as they explicitly discussed the issue, but even more importantly as they implicitly modeled it through their lives and ministries.

Extremely competent. Each woman included in my research is exceedingly competent in her profession. Whether serving or leading as volunteers, or serving as medical missionaries, church planters, program directors, executive leaders, or board members, the women regularly commented on how excellence provided credibility for their ministries and the gospel message they were seeking to convey.

They explained how a woman leading in God's mission receives respect because "she has done her work well." They said if our work speaks, if it is in line with what we say, it impacts everyone around us in positive ways. They tended to have little regard or respect for men or women who work in God's mission but do not seek to be excellent. To do poor-quality work and not care was deeply contradictory to their personal and professional values. They felt that people not committed to becoming excellent in their work should not get involved because leading in God's mission without that foundation hurts the cause of Christ. They were especially dismayed when people "ministered" in other nations under the guise of being a professional, but the quality of their work was poor. They simply could not understand that way of working.

As I reflected on many of their paths and the character they displayed in their ministries, I found myself often thinking about passages in Proverbs that talk a great deal about God's desire that we work with diligent hands. Proverbs 22:29 specifically came to mind. It highlights that a person's excellence in their work creates opportunities for significant influence. The women of this study are respected and were recommended to be part of the research because their work is held in such high esteem.

Committed to lifelong growth. It was fascinating to hear how their desire for excellence caused them to seek opportunities for continuing education and ongoing growth. For example, Aesha from South Asia said, "Be a lifelong learner. Be willing to admit failure and be willing to learn from anyone." Joan was born and raised in New Zealand, and her work trajectory has changed significantly over the years. She committed to "maintain a standard of excellence in professionalism, in conduct, using professional knowledge and skills in order to earn credibility in ministry." She said, "This meant I needed to continually upgrade my skills to carry out my ministry responsibilities." Over the course of her professional journey she has changed careers often, being willing to get new academic degrees to fruitfully tackle pressing needs her mission organization was facing.

These women believe developing themselves enables them to make their best contribution in God's mission in the world. Madison described how important this was to her. She said, "Seasons of waiting are for a purpose. I learned not to take it for granted. One of the things I did during that time was ask, what do I love doing? I grew my skill set. I learned more about my own gifts and my own passions so when the time came I was better equipped." So even when these women found themselves in difficult circumstances and the path before them was not always clear, they chose to focus on growing their skills and abilities so they might be prepared in the future when new ministry doors might open for them. They prepared to be excellent even when the path ahead was not yet certain.

Excellence Breaks Gender Biases

As these women commit to a path of excellence, new doors of leadership and influence open for them. At times, the very nature of their giftedness, and what they are able to contribute to a community because of their faithfulness in growing and developing the gifts that God has entrusted to them, breaks down the barriers normally faced by women. Excellence enables them to lead in ways that might not usually be possible because of their gender.

Discussion Questions:

1. What ministry outcomes are important for you to see when you invest your time and resources in mission?

2. What things cause you to get discouraged and wonder if you should keep investing your time and talents when you volunteer or work in a ministry?

3. What does excellence look like in your school, work, or ministry context?

4. In what ways do you sense God might want you to grow so you can be more excellent and have greater influence with others in your life now or in the years ahead?

PART THREE

REALITIES OF GENDER DISCRIMINATION

CARING ABOUT CHALLENGES

When we go back to our supporting church in the United States,
all the women meet in one room and the men in another. And
I find myself spending most of the time in the hallway.

HANNAH HAS SERVED FOR MANY YEARS AS A SENIOR
VICE PRESIDENT FOR A MISSION ALLIANCE WORKING
IN MORE THAN SIXTY NATIONS[1]

Yi-Ling is Singaporean. At work she is a strategic thinker, leading and making all kinds of decisions for her mission, carefully considering long-term implications, ripple effects, and so forth. But her church teaches that she needs to submit to male leadership at home, and it's hard when she sees unwise decisions being made that actually hurt the family. Her church says that a godly woman is supposed to be silent and submissive. For this reason she said,

> Whatever my husband wants, whatever my brothers say, for family harmony just let it go—as long as it's not too wrong. As long as it's not against God's standards, then I say I will just close my eyes and let it go. So that's a struggle. That is a real struggle for me. I think I've been expanded like a rubber band. And it's really hard to go back to the original shape. I think I've been stretched. Yeah.

Some might say if Yi-Ling never developed such strong leadership skills in the workplace, she would not be struggling so much at home. But the gifts of leadership often are there regardless of where a person lives or serves. If God creates and blesses a woman to be a strategic thinker, it is simply part of who she is, and it will keep manifesting itself. Gender stereotypes and restrictions create significant challenges if they do not permit her to express the wisdom God has put in her heart.

Potential for Misunderstanding

As we begin to address the topic of gender discrimination, let me be clear: I do not believe in male bashing, and neither do the women in this research. It is scripturally wrong to demean people based on their gender—whether they are male or female. It is also wrong to thrust on *every* man the anger and hurt caused by the actions of *some* men. While women in this book shared a number of hurtful situations, they also regularly spoke about many men who encouraged them in their ministry journeys. They spoke of guys who were extraordinary mentors, and men who opened up amazing leadership opportunities for them. They spoke at times of fathers, brothers, and male colleagues and bosses who modeled for them exemplary ways to lead, and they felt they owed each of these men a debt of gratitude for helping them to become the fruitful and effective ministry leaders they are today. This was expressed by many of the women, and I want to be explicit about that sentiment before proceeding into the challenges addressed in the next few chapters. There are countless kind men out there who genuinely care about women and the contributions they can make and are making in God's mission.

Metaphors They Expressed

Although there is a tremendous amount of kindness being extended to women by vast numbers of men, many women still face unique challenges, and it is important to understand and genuinely care about what they are encountering. Many metaphors the women shared are insightful. Yi-Ling's idea that she felt like a rubber band that kept being stretched helped to capture the stress they experience as they go back and forth between their workplaces, homes, churches, and communities. What women can and cannot do changes dramatically within the course of any given day depending on the different environments they inhabit. A European leader talked of having to learn how to "live in the in-between."

The in-between is between two extremes, you know? In society the pendulum has gone to one era, to the left with feminist theology and gender issues. And they have loud, loud voices. You know? For example we even have a Bible in "just" language alternating male and female pronouns for God. It's a very big lobby. On the other hand a good portion of denominations are still holding on to the idea that women should be silent, almost. They are not to be involved in leading a church.

So, depending on where you have been brought up, it's very hard to shed cultural messages and find your own path without ending up in the pendulum to the left or right. Living in the middle ground, in a self-assured, God-assured "happy almost" way. That is the challenge today. Yeah. How to navigate in-between those.

A couple of the women referred to themselves as "odd ducks" because how God has shaped them doesn't fit their church's narrow pictures of what women are supposed to be and do.

Sophia leads in publishing in North America. She said, "It always struck me as really odd. They say a woman may not teach, yet we teach in all sorts of ways. But we do an evangelical tap dance to find things that suit men theologically. But there is a fair element of hypocrisy in it at times." She said, "There are a lot of gymnastics we do around trying to keep our structures" so male colleagues will be okay with the idea of women being in the ministry workplace.

Sophia mentors respected theologians. She helps some of the leading theological minds in different regions of the globe sharpen their thinking so they can communicate to a wider, global audience. Yet the week before interviewing her for this book, Sophia casually mentioned in an email with fellow church members that it might be time for the congregation to consider having a woman on the board. She said her pastor, who rarely answers emails, showed up on her doorstep the very next day. He said if she chose to advocate for having a woman on the board, he would put all his energy into fighting her. She said she didn't want to fight, so she never mentioned the issue again.

What Discourages Women?

The following points are some of the situations and scenarios that discourage the women in this research. These things have weighed on their hearts, and they wished situations like this never happened or were far less common.

Experiences outside the workplace. In their personal life some of the women mentioned being physically abused by men at different times in their lives. Others spoke of years of psychological torment and taunting. Others experienced sexual abuse. This isn't surprising given that abuse against women is so common around the world. As Ellie very appropriately said after reflecting on what she had experienced, "Terrible things happen, but those are not God things. It is not God's heart for a woman to be abused." I wholly agree. There is simply no excuse, ever, for abuse. It never models God's heart for his daughters.

In addition to these issues, women also mentioned the challenge of carrying the larger share of the load whenever a family crisis or emergency arises. They are often the primary person caring for a sick child, a sick parent, or a struggling relative. Across the globe people often expect women to sacrifice their professional roles and aspirations for the needs of the people around them. In places where it was too expensive to pay others to help around the home, many women carried the additional weight of doing the household chores, while most of the men in similar professional roles had wives at home who did these things for them.

Experiences in the workplace. In their professional lives and workplaces, women leaders mentioned a variety of discouraging scenarios. The following were mentioned most frequently.

Compensation. Many talked about extreme financial disparities in their pay, simply because they were women. This often occurred regardless of the level of professionalism they exemplified in the workplace or the outcomes they were seeing through their leadership. Some said as soon as a ministry role came with a high salary, a robust benefit package, status, or prestige, a man would get that position even if women led at all other levels within the organization or ministry.

Promotions. Megan explained how frustrated she was with the double standards used when people are considered for promotions. For example, she said if a "guy has soft skills such as good relational competencies, he is considered to be an 'extraordinary leader.' But if women bring these same 'extraordinary qualities' to the table, it is merely expected because of their gender." Rachel served in a variety of significant executive leadership team roles for years. She was told by a leader in her organization to let her name stand in the executive director search, a job she felt well equipped for and called to do. However, immediately after making this comment, her male colleague said she would never get it because she was a woman, but he wanted her to let her name stand so the organization could tell the public they did consider women for the role. She was told her personality did not suit her for the job, yet her character traits were common and often seen as strengths in executive male leaders. She was later told he was joking, but it is hard to fully comprehend why anyone would think such a statement was funny.

Invisibility. Being treated like you are invisible can be incredibly hurtful, especially when women have served faithfully and worked so hard to be excellent leaders. Some women spoke about how frustrating it was that even though their own colleagues supported their leadership roles, when they were in meetings with men from other churches or ministries, often those guys would never address them or even look at them. They would only talk to other men in the room. Women from North America who were working with North American men from other ministries raised this issue about invisibility in meetings most frequently.

Patricia spoke of being in a senior executive role where a male colleague would not copy her on emails, even though they pertained to her. He wrote only to her subordinate, who is male, and that male subordinate told her what her colleague, who is her organizational peer, said. Others were always passed over for being mentored exclusively because of their gender. Therefore men around them would experience significant leaps in their development as leaders while women were invisible on the sidelines, never having what they needed to fully develop to their potential. Others spoke of how their ideas were stolen and used by men to get promotions or recognition.

A regular theme in their comments was deep frustration and irritation about going to large mission conferences and seeing only men leading plenary sessions. This was especially frustrating given women's pioneering work in global mission and the fact that more than half of the missionaries around the world are women. I have wrestled with this as well. It is also frustrating to be a woman leader at these types of gatherings when people assume you are an executive director's spouse or his administrative assistant, instead of someone who is fully participating in the event as a leader.

Proving themselves. An overwhelming theme in many women's comments was feeling like they relentlessly had to keep proving themselves over and over again. Several said they were tired that they had to keep doing this because of their gender. If they were the first women in leadership roles in organizations, the pressure was even greater. I understand these comments because I have felt the same weight over the years. Women in leadership often have to perform far better than men to be assessed or evaluated as equal to or as good as male peers. They often must perform far better than men in similar roles or they risk hurting all the women coming behind them. I have often experienced this pressure in speaking engagements at conferences, and I feel I have to invest far more time preparing than most of the men I know because the work will be judged differently. What I do has to be extraordinary to be seen and heard.

Shu-Ching experienced this dynamic in a different way: "Since I am a woman of color, an immigrant from Asia, and receiving Westernized theological and leadership training, my identity and my call have been sometimes a blessing and sometimes a challenge to any community I serve. I have encountered either high expectations or low expectations from people I have served." What she rarely faces are normal expectations. She said, "They like my preaching, but they wish I were a man." Nicole, a young leader from Africa, also felt this relentless pressure because of her gender and the color of her skin:

> As an African there is a very obvious constant something that hovers over you, that you are not good enough. That you are not effective enough. You have to prove a point. I don't know to whom. And even sometimes when people are talking there is a lot of patronizing talk that is very well meaning. Sometimes leaders say, "We need to open the table." Who said the table was yours to open? So they say, "Let's open the space. Let's allow the people." Who are you to be the one who is "allowing"? You know? It's just so difficult, that whole colonial, racist reality.

So this need to prove oneself often intensifies in some ministry settings where there are women of color.

Dizzying Inconsistencies in Churches

Until I did this research, I don't think I absorbed how dizzying, wholly inconsistent, and often illogical all of the gender restrictions are for women in different churches and ministries. For example, within this relatively small sample, women from the same denomination often experienced different restrictions. Within one denomination some could preach, but they could not preside over the Eucharist. Others could not preach or lead in any way if a man was present, and others could perform all clergy responsibilities, including being the equivalent of a senior or sole pastor at a church. In some seminaries women could lead as professors and be integrally involved in the pastoral-formation process for men, but they might not be permitted to lead a simple mix-gendered Bible class or small group at their local congregation. In another seminary a woman could have planted a large number of thriving churches, but later in life when she came to seminary she would be told, "It's like Deborah's time. You can't be doing that. There are now men to do that."

Some are told they can "share," but they can never "preach." Others can talk in front of the podium but never behind the podium. Others can perform an extensive spectrum of ministerial functions, as long as it is done under the rubric of being "the pastor's wife." In those situations, as long as what she is doing is not documented in a job description and she is not being paid, it is permissible. In some instances women can be evangelists and prophets, but they might not be permitted to preach. I'm still not sure what that difference is, because what they tend to say in each role seems to be the same. Some are allowed to baptize new converts to the faith. Others are told they can never baptize, because that is a man's role. In some churches women can be involved in public prayers, read passages of Scripture, take offerings, assist with Communion, and the like, but in other congregations only men are allowed to do those things.

It varies as well in nonprofit ministries. Nicole, the young African leader just referenced, told me that in one country in Africa the executive director, who is also a woman, is not permitted to lead prayer at a board meeting. However, when it is her turn to speak, this female executive director gives her report, and it is clear that she is deeply respected and runs the entire organization quite well. Nicole said, "In our country in Kenya, women can pray in board meetings but there you can't." Women serving as executive directors for ministries that work with a broad spectrum of denominations and churches have their work cut out for them trying to discern what is permissible and what is not because of their gender.

Navigating These Things

Often what women can and cannot do in ministry leadership roles fluctuates tremendously, changing significantly among churches within the same denomination and even between churches in the same city. In other instances it fluctuates and can change radically within a single congregation or ministry, depending on who the next senior pastor or executive director might be. *For these reasons many women regularly experience the landscape shaking under their feet, wondering at any given time if what they can or cannot do will now be prohibited, encouraged, marginalized, or no longer funded.*

However, what struck me the most with these women was how gracefully they dealt with the various gender obstacles they were facing. While some were still struggling with feelings of anger and frustration, which is legitimate given what they had experienced, the overwhelming majority found a way forward by implementing a variety of strategies they believed were serving them well. What follows in the next two chapters is not meant to imply that these are the best strategies to employ; nor is it to be taken as a statement that gender discrimination should not be addressed directly in all its various forms. Instead, it is an opportunity to share what these women found helpful in their diverse circumstances, cultures and ministry contexts.

Discussion Questions

1. What limitations, if any, do women face in your work or ministry context?

2. What encourages, confuses, or discourages you about what you see in terms of what women can or cannot do in your context?

3. How do you see women responding to gender challenges or obstacles they face?

4. How do you respond when you face challenges or obstacles that seem unfair or illogical?

CHAPTER NINE

STRATEGIES THAT ACCOMMODATE OTHERS

In my culture, women play a backdoor role, meaning that their point of view is important, but people don't see them on the scene. For example, when a chief says that "the night will bring advice," it means that he will seek advice from his first wife. The society does not give women a leading role. The expectations that people have of women leaders are to be discreet, nondominant. They are very different from the expectations that the society has vis-à-vis men.

ALIMA IS FROM FRANCOPHONE WEST AFRICA AND
HAS SPENT MUCH OF HER LIFE IN LEADERSHIP
ROLES TO INCREASE LITERACY LEVELS AMONG
MARGINALIZED PEOPLE GROUPS[1]

Megan is a leader in North America who was overseeing a team in an academic institution. She explained that she had a female voice, a PhD credential, and a strong education and mission background. Her colleague who reported to her helped to lead the department, and he had a male voice, a seminary degree, and was a person of color. She said,

> Before we would think about how we wanted to influence we would say, "Which of us is the best person to go into that space?" Because the point is not to make a point about who is

in charge. The point was to use our common language to persuade others toward a goal that furthered the missional purpose.

So, sometimes it would be my male colleague and sometimes it would be me. What is going to be heard here? Is it the higher position? Is it the doctorate? Is it the MDiv degree? Is it being a person of color? Is it being male? So we would divide and conquer, and that allowed us to be very flexible in how things got done.

Because she and her male colleague worked very well together, the strategy was fruitful.

Living in a Complicated World

Women regularly find themselves having to navigate a wide array of diverse circumstances and contexts. For some, if their ministry calling fits within cultural gender norms, they can experience greater consistency as they move between family, ministry, church, and societal roles. However, many women around the globe frequently have to make choices about which strategies they will use as they face obstacles in a variety of settings because of differing expectations about what women can or cannot do.

It is easy to stand outside of another's context and judge a strategy as being inappropriate. Some believe accommodation should never be made for any structure or expectation that is unfair or unjust. However, after meeting so many people in a wide array of diverse countries, cultures, ministries, and families, I have come to the personal conclusion that often a variety of strategies are needed to navigate complexities faced regularly by women serving and leading in God's mission. Sometimes strategies of accommodation further God's purposes, and they can be employed in a variety of ways. The following are some of the accommodations strategies they mentioned.

Allowing the offended person to work with a man. While gender discrimination can be extremely painful, some women have chosen to accommodate a person who believes it is only appropriate to work with a man. For example, Isabella was the general secretary of her mission organization in Latin America, which means she was the national leader for the ministry. She said many men helped her over the years, but she occasionally ran into gender barriers. She said, "Sometimes for the pastors, the old pastors, it was a problem. But many churches opened the door for the movement—maybe not for me but for the movement. I could ask many men from the movement to go to preach at other churches, and to present the movement at those churches. It was a nice time for me." When Isabella ran into these hurdles she said, "I understand. It's not about me. It's about the kingdom of God. It's about the movement. So, okay, you don't want me? No problem. I'll send you another guy, a man. No problem. It's not about me."

Patricia has served as a vice president and in other senior roles in mission organizations. She spoke of the issue of reporting relationships. Sometimes during her career leading in God's mission she has encountered men who seemed unable to accept a female boss. She said, "That can become very challenging. And one of the strategies I've used is to inject between myself and that person another level of leadership, if possible, so that it's not a direct concern." She explained that she also adds these men to the top of her prayer list to better ensure that the attitude of her heart toward them stays in a good place.

Submitting when men assume full spiritual responsibility. Some women are willing to accommodate a gender prohibition and not serve or lead in a specific way *if* the man making the request is wholly willing to assume the full weight of spiritual accountability for and repercussions of what will not happen in the kingdom if she does not do what God is requesting. Amber shared her story about this: "I grew up with a stepfather who didn't believe women should be leaders. He was very strong about that. So, when I went to Bible school, my parents thought that was good for everyone, for a year, just to get a good spiritual foundation before you go on to do something else." She said they grudgingly agreed to let her go back to Bible school for a second year, but the crisis arose when she said she wanted to go back for a third year to get a theology degree. "My stepfather wanted to know what I would do with that, and I said that I would pastor. He put his foot down. He forbade me to go back."

Amber said her parents were fine with her going for more schooling to lead in any other area of life, as long as it wasn't in a church. She continued,

> Yet after my mom died, I discovered through my aunt and through some of her journals that she always knew that I would be a pastor. The Lord spoke to her. She [my mom] had become a Christian when she was pregnant with me. It's a long story, but for her it was—this is what this child is headed toward.
>
> So anyway, coming back to this conversation with my stepdad. I was nineteen years old. I was very zealous for the Lord, and I just took the Lord at face value. And I went to my stepfather. You can imagine we had a fairly complicated relationship. It was abusive, and not without its complications. There was domestic violence and things.

But I went to him and said, "Dad, I'm wondering if we could just pray and even fast if you feel led to over the week, and then next week can we talk about it and discuss what we heard from the Holy Spirit—whether I go back to school or not." And he said "okay," because that sounded very spiritual to him.

So I was very intentional about it. I prayed and I did a bit of fasting, and I tried to listen. I felt like I was supposed to go to Bible school. And so the following week I went to him and said, "What did you sense, or what did you hear from the Lord?" He said to me, "Well, I haven't really heard anything, but I haven't changed my position. You know, Paul seems very clear to me: 'I don't permit a woman to teach.' So, that's the way it is."

I said, "Okay. Here is the thing. As near as I can discern I have to obey my heavenly Father. But I also have this call to honor my parents. And so, I'm kind of betwixt and between what I'm to do. So, I'll tell you what. I can submit and obey what you say as long as you are willing to be responsible for what I don't do in the kingdom. So, if you can say with surety that you will accept any responsibility—in case I am genuinely called and I don't do the things I was created to do. I'll find other things to do. But if I don't do those things, you will answer to the Lord for those things.

"I feel very clear that I have heard from the Holy Spirit about a call to pastor, so if I don't do it you have to accept responsibility. Right? I have to obey my heavenly Father over you. But I need to be obedient to you. I'm not trying to be rebellious. I'm actually trying really hard to obey both of you."

He replied, "Fine then. Go back to school. I can't be 100 percent sure."

She said her stepfather did not go to her graduation or ordination or to hear her preach even though she went on to become a famous preacher in her nation. But years later, after her mom died and her stepfather remarried, Amber was invited to preach at his church. After hearing her message, he joined the long line of people waiting to talk with her. When he reached the front he told her, "This was right and good. God is obviously doing something that I did not understand or know." Amber said, "That is all he ever said about it, but to me that was a *huge* moment to realize I had done both. I had tried to honor him and I had obeyed the Lord. And it didn't have to create animosity. It didn't mean he was full of blessing, and showing up and supportive. But I could just faithfully walk that path quietly, and he could see the fruit of it much later."

Assuming good intentions while responding graciously. Victoria is a young leader who has navigated gender bias in a few different spheres of ministry, yet she seems to weather these situations with a great deal of grace. Her approach has proven to be helpful for her personally and also for others in the communities she has served. She said,

> Having confidence is important. Where there are moments when you know it is strategic and you can speak, speak. Because if you don't, that might be the only opportunity you have to bring something to light. To say, "You know what, have you thought about what it might look like if a woman attends this or this or this?" Sometimes it just takes saying something, and you are the one who is going to have that perspective. Nobody else in the room is. It might not be deliberate or intentional, they've just done what they've always done.

With an easygoing approach in which she starts by believing people do not mean to be harmful, she can sometimes help people to recognize gender blind spots they might have held for years.

Theresa works in correctional ministries and has also led in other ministry settings. She struggles at times with the conversation about gender discrimination.

> I think it can be distracting if you focus on the fact that you are woman leader, because then you begin to look at things that marginalize you or discriminate against you. Whatever you look for, that's what you find. I would say don't waste your time on that. Focus on being the best leader you can be, how God has gifted you, but also do not be afraid to speak up when there is marginalization or discrimination. Because I think a lot of times in some male-dominated areas or ministries they are not aware. They are not intentionally behaving in unhelpful ways. It's the culture or way of thinking. It's a way to educate men on how to lead women.
>
> So again, it's not out fighting a cause, but you are addressing the marginalizing behavior in a way that is respectful. Some-times it's not intentionally done. It's a lack of awareness and just operating in their own world. So, I think pointing out marginalization is helpful. I see leadership growth over the years. In my younger years I was just silent about discrimination. I just dealt with it. I didn't point it out. I didn't speak up about it. Now I would be a little more assertive in pointing out discrimination and marginality.

Ann likes to integrate humor in a fun way to raise awareness at times when she encounters gender discrimination. She believes the best of the person, but she will respond with a sly or funny comment to help them see the situation more clearly. She has held a number of leadership roles, is married to a pastor, has adult sons, and is highly educated. However, in a ministry job interview, she was asked if she could "talk to men." She shared how she addressed the biased question:

> I find the absurdity in life, and I can find some things laughable. Also being playful with it. I've often used humor, like in that setting where I was asked if I could speak to men. With a grin and a sparkle in my eye I said, "Well I'm speaking to you aren't I?" And it lightens the mood, but it also makes a point. So, trying to own the dynamic, not in a way that makes someone feel small, but yet still playfully gets the point across.

For these women the point is not to humiliate or shame men, or make them feel small, because they realize that often men are not intentional when harmful things are said or done. They realize that many truly spiritual and kind men in ministry workplaces say and do some weird things to women, but they genuinely have no malice in their hearts.

Accepting what they cannot change. Perhaps the most significant dynamic behind accommodation strategies when gender discrimination arises is the willingness for women to discern what is out of their control. They seem to understand what they can and cannot change. It does not mean that they appreciate or like gender discrimination. In quiet moments, unfair and unjust things they experience can cause deep frustration, tears, and prayers of lament before their heavenly Father. But the reality is that in so many contexts where women serve and lead, men determine what is and is not permissible.

Women often pay a steep price when they start confronting all the subtle and not so subtle discriminatory realities in their ministry contexts. At the least they will often gain the reputation for being a complainer or a difficult person, and when that happens their gifts and contributions usually are discounted or marginalized. They will be passed over for leading meaningful projects and starting new initiatives, even if the label is wholly unfair. In other situations, when women point out inconsistencies and hypocrisy, some men may feel uncomfortable and might take away the leadership platforms these women have developed through years of faithful service. If that happens the scope of what these woman can accomplish decreases substantially. I have chosen accommodation strategies many times over the years because I knew if I said anything about the inconsistencies, ministry opportunities would close for me. I worried about that as I wrote this book as well. Pointing out gender inconsistencies and injustice in ministry workplaces can easily make me a target for any number of unjust accusations and repercussions.

Sometimes women face genuine danger when they begin questioning gender injustices. For some, it might mean being ostracized by their families, becoming more vulnerable to physical and sexual abuse, or even being killed. Therefore, accommodation strategies do not arise out of a weakness of character, a lack of faith, or an unwillingness to stand up for justice. The situations women face around the globe are far more complex, and sometimes accommodation strategies are simply the wisest response when women have far less power in family, ministry, church, and social contexts.

Trusting God Will Make Things Right in the End

Realizing that God is more powerful helps when women face challenging instances or seasons of injustice. What we are seeing now is not what will always be. A day is coming when truth and justice will prevail, and God will make things right (Revelation 21–22). We can take heart that we are doing well if we choose to be part of the solution by becoming better people in the midst of gender challenges, and by using what power we do have to model Christlikeness.

In my research I have been astounded by this: when women encountering difficult gender hurdles choose forgiveness over bitterness, God often finds ways around the hurdles and gives them even more influence than if the original door they sought had been open to them. I've seen this time and again in my own life and in the lives of many others. God seems intent on giving human beings, be they men or women, ever greater influence if they remain faithful to him (Matthew 25:21).[2]

Discussion Questions

1. In what ways do you see women taking gender (or other) issues personally when they shouldn't?

2. How might giving a person the benefit of the doubt make it easier to navigate challenging situations in your work or ministry context?

3. In what ways does accommodating others align with or contradict messages in your culture?

4. One day God will make all things right. What impact might this truth have on you if you were encountering unfair or unjust circumstances?

CHAPTER TEN

WHEN ACCOMMODATION HINDERS FAITHFULNESS

So I think women are trying to be wise and use opportunities
that are open instead of fighting. That's my observation. That's
what I can say. Personally, I would prefer to do that. Personally,
I would prefer to use all opportunities that will open doors
for me to improve society. That's what I do.

SEMIRA IS ETHIOPIAN, AND SHE LEADS IN NETWORKS
THAT HELP AT-RISK CHILDREN, AND
SHE TRAINS FUTURE LEADERS[1]

*A*s a little girl, Idha was told she could not speak or ask questions in church because of her gender. When she grew older, she realized she could not accommodate that gender restriction and be faithful to God's calling on her life, so she left her family's denomination to be part of a congregation that enabled women to be more involved in ministry. She currently leads in a seminary and trains pastors. She said,

> How I've reconciled it to myself, the more conservative de-
> nominations, is I've always thought that denominations should
> have distinctives. So, this is the way they do things as long as
> you are in the denomination. I don't go shaking the boat. There
> are many other denominations that will suit you better. I would

rather move out of a denomination and find the one I'm most comfortable in, rather than stay where I am and try to reform it. I simply think to be a reformer is a big ask, and I'm not cut out to be that.

In my country, like I said, anything religious is still very heavily male dominated. Once in a while, in a rare while, I still chafe against that. I like to do work in church because that sort of keeps me grounded. I want to know where the problems are, how common people think, and how laypersons work out theology in their heads. So I like to teach in church. But sometimes I've found that those opportunities can be closed even in the church where I am now. It depends on which pastor is leading the church.

Idha explained that she left her parents' denomination so she could be more active in ministry in her church, and for many years that was possible. But her congregation recently received a new senior pastor, and he decided that because she is a woman she can no longer lead a small group with men and women who were deeply enjoying her teaching, even though that group was growing significantly. She realizes the new pastor likely feels threatened by her because she has much more theological education. She continued,

But you know, I've never let this stop me. It's like lightning. I try to follow the path of least resistance. So now I'm facing resistance about teaching Bible studies because I would be teaching male adults in the group. So what I've found over the summer is there is a place to teach teenagers. There was a summer school and now there is a Sunday school that starts up this month. And I offered to teach Sunday school for a change. This is something I haven't done for about twenty years now. I thought, *Well, if I can't do this, let me do the other one.*

Just because a door closes, I don't stand outside and kick it. That's a waste of my energy. I keep constantly looking for other doors that might be slightly ajar, and then I get my foot in, and I go do that. And these are all in my area of gifts. . . . Well, if it's not adults, let me teach children. And if it's not children, then I'll go to teens instead. Or I'll start a children's reading club in my neighborhood. I just keep creating opportunities for myself to serve.

And maybe I look at all of these as God-directed in some way. And so I don't get too frustrated about it. I know if God wanted me to serve there, he would open that door for me, even in spite of human systems. So it's just looking for opportunities and making myself comfortable wherever I am.

So regarding hindrances, there is culture. There is patriarchy all over the world. There is that. There are the egos of human beings. Women can have egos just as much as men. But there is human fault and failure, there is that. So the hindrances I am talking about are all universals, really, and it's all part of the fallenness of our world.

While Idha acknowledges the realities of gender obstacles and hurdles in her context, she does not let these prohibitions keep her from being active in serving and leading in God's mission. Instead, she takes full advantages of the opportunities that might exist to minister and develop her talents and skills for the good of others and the furtherance of God's purposes.

Strategies When the Stakes Are Too High

While a wide variety of gender barriers exist around the world, sometimes accommodating the needs and wishes of others is simply not possible because there are many instances when God's will does not align with those restrictions. To accommodate, therefore, would require that a woman or ministry no longer remain faithful to what they believe God is asking them to do. This is often a tense place when people see God's will and purposes differently; however, it happens regularly across the globe.

It is not uncommon for some women to sense that God is asking them to serve and lead in ways that deviate from stereotypical roles of women or even from church policies. In other instances a board or ministry might sense that God wants them to extend a service or leadership invitation to a particular woman, but not all of their donors or ministry partners would agree with that decision because they hold different cultural or theological views about what is and is not permissible for women. For these reasons, when accommodation is not an option or the repercussions of accommodation would hinder God's mission, the women in this research mentioned a variety of strategies they employed to find ways to continue growing and actively fulfilling what they sensed God was asking them to do.

Letting the offended person work it out. Alia was asked to be the first female executive director of a national ministry in Europe. Her colleagues and the board wanted her in the role and fully supported her. But many of the ministry's donors came from a variety of denominations that had different views about women serving and leading in mission. She said, "In my own organization, I always felt treated with respect and dignity. Almost like, 'Oh this is great. They welcomed me.' I felt like I was always welcomed as a female leader. So, it was more an attack from certain denominations that had problems with me in that leadership role. But generally I felt I was well-received and respected."

When Alia ran into conflict with those who thought a woman should not be leading the mission, she said,

I came to a firm conviction. If other people said they believed differently, I said I fully understand. I comprehend where you are coming from, but my own understanding is different. For example, one guy called and said he wanted to talk to the board because they made a big mistake putting me here. He wanted me to talk to the board because they should take me out of this position.

I said, "I don't think there is much chance of the board changing their mind, because they are the ones who wanted me there. And the membership wanted me here. I understand your dilemma. Our mission organization has a woman in leadership and you are against it. So you either have to say the work of this ministry is so important I will keep supporting that work, or you say the fact that there is a woman in leadership is such a terrible thing I have to stop supporting them. Then you give your support to another mission organization, and I'm sure they will like it. But this is up to you. You have to make a decision. It is not up to us." So, I gave it back to them, you know?

So, do you know what the guy did? He sent a donation and wrote, "For male missionaries only." I thought, *Look at him. He came up with an unusual solution*, and I thought, *Good for you!*

You know? I came to understand that for some people, it is such a terrible thought that a woman is in leadership, because they have been shaped in a certain way. And, to be honest, I never fought it. I never fought it, because I felt for them. I did not pity them, but I tried to understand. But I also gave it back to him. We can't solve it for you, but you have to solve it for yourself. It's multilayered.

In this way Alia was able to navigate challenges related to her role in the mission without becoming unduly upset. By responding with compassion and letting offended people wrestle with how to best respond, she was able to focus on the job she was given to do.

Letting God change a resistant heart. In her late twenties, Chelsea was in her first pastorate leading youth and young adults. At that time, she heard God saying to her repeatedly that she would be preaching to her whole nation. She recounted the story:

He said I would preach to the country, which was also a very radical and insane idea. I had actually been relegated in my first pastorate to youth and young adults. Even the young adults were a bit of a leap for them. But it was a megachurch. I felt this call to leave. I felt like the Lord told me that I would preach to the whole country. I had never even preached in my own church. I had never preached a Sunday to the congregation, so how was I going to preach to the whole country?

So I told the Lord, *If this is you*—because it kept coming to me whenever I would pray—*If this is you, go ahead and knock yourself out.* I heard in prayer that I would preach in the capital of our country. I would start there, and after that I would preach to the whole country. And I thought, *If this is you, knock yourself out. If not, I'm going to pretend I never heard it.* There was no way humanly that I could ever make that happen.

And the following week I received a phone call inviting me to preach at a church in my country's capital. And I got asked to do a youth retreat, but I got asked to preach at that church on the Sunday evening after the retreat. So, if you want to speak in terms of getting to preach to adults, then this was my first chance since graduating.

But anyway, I did it. I knew exactly what I was supposed to preach. It was about six weeks later that I went. I preached, and at the end I didn't have any clue how to do an altar call or response. So I decided I better pray. With my eyes closed, I invited the Holy Spirit to show us how we should respond, and about 650 people hit the floor. I think a spirit of repentance came over people, and they laid down on their faces and wept.

And I was shocked! I opened my eyes because I heard a lot of noise. And I realized what was happening and I thought, *I want to get out of the way because I don't know what to do with this.* So, then I knew I really would go and preach to the country. I really knew it was the Lord, but it was another year before that happened.

After several months serving as the youth and young adult pastor at her church, Chelsea talked to her senior pastor and explained that she sensed God was asking her to leave. She said, "I told him I thought I should preach to the country," and he listened. She explained that it was a church model where she had supervising pastors, and because the congregation was over five thousand members, she had only met with the senior pastor five times in seven years. She said, "So, I met with him and told him this was coming, and that I was going to obey the Lord and I was going to go. And I wanted to give them enough time to figure out what they were going to do for a replacement."

She explained that he went away to speak at a retreat that weekend, and left her a letter in her church mailbox. She said after reading it:

I went home and cried my eyes out, because the letter basically said, "I'm not going to have a 'your word of the Lord' versus 'my word of the Lord' argument. These are thirteen reasons why you are not to leave, and I am your covering." This was the kind of language, "Because I'm the senior pastor and you are a woman." It was really quite condescending actually. And I just so much wanted to please the Lord and do the right thing and be obedient, and not fight for my place as a woman. And I didn't know how to respond to this. I went to a couple of friends for advice, and they had no idea.

And I prayed that whole weekend, and I felt like the Lord told me to be silent, which was the oddest thing because, you might have caught on, I'm quite a verbose individual! So the next week, on the Tuesday, I was at work and I got a call from his secretary asking me to come and meet with him, and so I did. And he said, "I wonder if you got my letter." I said I did. And he said, "What were your thoughts?"

Now I'm supposed to be silent, right? So I said, "I'm very thankful for your willingness to speak what you think and to share from your heart, and I have a lot of respect for you." And then I stopped there. And it kind of went back and forth a bit, and finally he said, "Are you going to say anything?" And I said. "Actually, I feel like I'm supposed to be silent." And I just sat there like an idiot, you know?

And then he began to cry. And he said the Lord woke him up at the retreat where he had gone to preach over the weekend and told him he was wrong, but that he was only to release me if I was silent. So I felt like I passed this mega-test in the school of the Spirit.

And so then he wanted to make a way for me. He said, "Can I write a letter to all the district offices and recommend you as a speaker?" And I said, "No. I don't think any human person is supposed to open the door for me. I think the Lord is going to do it. I need him to do it, so I know it's him."

Since that time Chelsea has traveled and preached throughout her nation, in every province except the least populated and most remote one, and in all the major cities. Her ministry is quite remarkable; I've never seen anything like it. Denominations and ministries that normally don't talk with one another have all welcomed her with open arms. She regularly speaks at large conferences alongside some of the most respected ministry leaders and seminary presidents in her nation. It's simply amazing.

Graciously accepting a new ministry assignment. Adriana was always the leader of her youth movement at her church in South America, and all of her peers assumed she would also be their national president. She said,

But in the election, the president said, "Okay, we will choose the president. But the president is a 'he' because we need to be led by a man. So, it's very important." So all the people were—ooh. Because it's weird, no? It was, "Why? Adriana is our leader! Why is it she can't do that?"

That was hard for me. I was praying. I was saying, If God allowed that, it is okay for me. But I was in a struggle with the leadership of the church. I started to pray again. I said to God, "If you give me these gifts, put me in a place where I can use them."

So, at that time in the youth movement they invited me to come to the capital city and work as a staff worker. And that was great because I could leave my church, my original church, very nice, without big problems. And that church is my parents' church. So it's important that it be a good connection, yes?

When she moved she became a part of the church where she now serves with her husband. She said, "And they opened the doors for me to teach, to preach. That was amazing because I really feel that God responded to my prayer." Adriana said God spoke to her heart and said, "Okay, you want a place. There's your place. Go in!" She said, "I really appreciate that from God."

Advice to younger women. Two of the women shared thoughts they give to younger women who are wrestling with gender obstacles. In both instances they recommended that young women be honest about the impact of staying versus going, encouraging more the latter. Felecia is African American with a trusted record leading in biblical-social justice and community development. She said,

So that's been my role. The last ten years or so I've mentored more women than I ever would have thought God would give to me. I realize sometimes it is just walking with them, listening to them, saying, "Have you thought about this? Here is the opportunity. Are you ready to pay the price for what it will cost to push this door open for other people?" So just setting them up to be realistic about how difficult this might be. Or just saying there is an easier door, go that way. Challenging them to see what God has for them and if they fail, fail up.

Annette had strong feelings about this as well. She said, "Women should not let themselves be bullied or abused in a work situation." She recommended that they leverage what they could from a bad experiences and move on or "spiral up." She felt they needed to leave and go someplace where they could make a contribution and do the work God was calling them to do.

Sensitivity Required When Verbalizing Issues

Theresa commented that she often saw women leaving ministries when they encountered gender discrimination. Frequently they do not say the real reasons why they are leaving; they give other excuses. She felt this was inappropriate and that they should be honest; otherwise there is no organizational learning. However, leaving a job and saying it is because of gender discrimination can be quite risky. If you are already hurt because you feel disrespected because of your gender, voicing concern in that environment can lead to a number of unpleasant outcomes. Some people might fear that you will take them to court. When that happens, the human resources department of many organizations will start circling you to manage the problem, often in ways that leave an exiting colleague feeling even more wounded.

For these reasons, and because at times people do not want blind spots pointed out or truth to be voiced, speaking about gender discrimination in work places requires a great deal of discernment. It is easiest to do it when things are going well rather than at times of conflict or when you are leaving to work somewhere else. Women need to keep in mind their larger goals and discern if the backlash that might arise is worth what they are likely to gain from such a confrontation. I believe it is for this reason most women simply leave and never voice the real reasons for their departures from ministries.

They Don't Want to Fight

Several women mentioned leaving ministries because there was no way to exercise the gifts God had given them. They felt accountable to find ways to use their gifts and talents in churches and ministries because burying them was not an option (see Matthew 25:14-30). However, a consistent thread in these stories is their strong desire to not fight about gender obstacles and restrictions they were facing in ministry. These women did not want to cause divisions or hurt relationships. One woman's comment seemed to capture the essence of how many felt: "It's an issue I care about passionately, but I'm not a fighter." They don't want to tear down people or ministries. I found this to be both inspiring and a bit heartbreaking. They are concerned about the well-being of others and about not causing division or disruption for church leaders. However, I'm not sure if that same level of care is as readily extended to them.

Discussion Questions

1. How do you respond when someone is offended by what you sense God is asking you to do?

2. Would you prefer to stay and fight for change or go to a different workplace where injustices you might be facing will no longer be a problem?

3. Under what circumstances do you think it is best for a person to leave in order to serve in a different workplace or ministry?

4. What advice would you give to a friend who is considering leaving a workplace or ministry because they are not seeing how they can use their gifts in that context?

PART FOUR

WHAT WOMEN NEED TO DO THEIR BEST WORK

CHAPTER ELEVEN

IF MARRIED, HUSBANDS WHO ACT LIKE JESUS

*I felt badly that I had been traveling and been gone so much because
of ministry trips, and I apologized to my husband. He gave me a
big hug and told me not to worry. He said he made a commitment
to God when we got married that he never wanted to stand in the
way of how God wanted to use me. He said he was proud of me!*

MARY IS NORTH AMERICAN AND A MISSIOLOGIST
WHO CONDUCTS RESEARCH AND WORKS WITH
GLOBAL LEADERS TO ADDRESS ISSUES
THAT ARE HINDERING MINISTRY[1]

Julia, a South African, believes her husband's support and encouragement has had a significant impact in her development and her ability to continue in her leadership position.

> From the outset, my husband gave his blessing to my appointment
> to a position of leadership. He encouraged me to accept the
> challenge for the love of God's mission and for his glory. Seeing
> my eagerness to serve and support him, my husband goes out
> of his way to accommodate and support me, and so we both
> thrive in our respective ministries. I suspect that had I taken
> the hard line of pulling rank, as it were, one of us would almost
> certainly have had to step down from our leadership position,

thus forfeiting the demonstrated truth and beauty of mutual support in the face of the heavy demands of leadership.

Without the support of my husband, I would not have lasted long in my current leadership role. In my desire to steward what has been entrusted to me, I draw strength and peace from knowing I have God's approval, as well as that of my husband. In addition, the backing of the board and fellow colleagues on the leadership team is invaluable to me as a woman in leadership. Without their covering I would be very vulnerable to discouragement and inordinate strain.

Many of the chapters in this book are focused on the actions these women take to remain faithful and connected in their leadership. As a whole, they tend to assume a great deal of personal responsibility for whether things go well or poorly; however, in listening to their stories, it became evident that there are limits to what they can personally change. To fully accomplish God's purposes in the world and do their best work in ministry requires help and support from others. Approximately one-third of the women in this research are single, and they had supportive friends who helped them on their journeys. However, if the women are married, their husbands' responses make a significant difference when God extends invitations to serve and lead.

Are They Married to the Same Guy?

A shocking result of my research is that the women I interviewed seemed to be married to the same guy! It was uncanny how they tended to describe their husbands in the same ways. However, I knew some of their husbands, and outwardly they did not seem similar to me at all. Some were shy and quiet, while others were talkative and outgoing. Some were ministry leaders, while others worked in supporting ministry roles such as IT or finance. And others were in businesses not related to ministry. However, as I analyzed the data, they seemed to share five traits: (1) none of these husbands seemed focused primarily on his own comfort; (2) none seemed to be competing with his wife; (3) none appeared threatened by her success; (4) each of them seemed to wholly support and encourage his wife to grow to her full potential; and (5) each seemed to take genuine joy in his wife's accomplishments.

As I worked my way through the interviewing process, what concerned me most was that these accomplished women did not mention other types of husbands. Many exceptional single women lead in God's mission. However, I wondered whether the married women who fully develop and remain in leadership roles for long periods of times are only those who have this same type of husband.

That tentative hypothesis seemed to bear out toward the end of the research when a young and especially gifted leader broke down in tears before me. Through sobs she said she didn't know how she could be a good leader *and* a good wife and mom. Her husband was not happy, and marital conflict was causing her to consider not being a leader any more. Another young leader who works with the homeless was asked what she thought women needed in order to do their best work in ministry. She answered, "A personal sense of calling into the ministry coupled with the knowledge that your husband fully agrees with you filling a leadership position." Another said, "If you are married, step into the ministry only if your husband agrees."

Even if a husband is not supportive, it is still possible for a married woman to lead in God's mission. However, after completing this research, it is my belief that if he is not the type of husband described in the following pages, a married woman's leadership journey will be far more difficult.

The Marriage Mystery

Scripture teaches that a couple's marriage relationship should reflect the mystery of Christ's relationship with his bride, the church (Ephesians 5:22-33). The women in this research justifiably felt the weight of being true to their marriage vows and covenant. They did not want to harm their husbands or their children. These women yearned to be faithful. However, as I pondered what the women were saying I found myself reflecting on this mystery of Christ and his bride, and what that might mean. If in marriage we are called to reflect such a mystery, it warrants considering a number of critical questions for husbands. Each has significant bearing on the topic of married women leading in God's mission, because the answers to these are often far more countercultural in faith communities than we might at first imagine.

Does Jesus focus on his own comfort? In many cultures and families around the world, a chief concern is the husband's comfort. In some cultures this means a wife must focus on cooking meals he likes, making sure his home is clean, ensuring his children are well-behaved, and responding to his sexual desires. This is often how people view marriage, and many women are happy in this kind of relationship. However, a common metaphor in certain parts of the world is that a husband should be "king of his castle." A husband should be able to call all the shots, and not have to put aside his wants and needs, which a good wife should attend to. In many cultures men are able to divorce their wives if they become unhappy with them. Sadly, statistics reveal when this is taken too far, there are alarming rates of physical, psychological, and sexual abuse.

But is life about comfort? As we look at Scripture, Jesus does not seem to be focused on having his bride meet all of his comfort needs. That is not the role of the bride of Christ. Many of the women in my research are such fruitful leaders because their husbands are not focused on having all of their personal desires and creature comforts met. For example, Danielle said, "I have a husband who says he supports me in this. He said, 'I don't necessarily like it when you are away, but this is what God has called you to do. This is the gift he has given to you. He is using you, and I support that.'" Havilah said, "When I began doctoral studies abroad, my mother-in-law moved in to take care of the home. When she was no longer able to do that, my husband stepped in. With admirable speed he went from not being able to boil an egg to dishing out pepper-fried mutton." This research has caused me to reflect on whether focusing on a husband's comfort accurately models the marriage mystery Christ calls us to.

Is Jesus threatened by his bride? When I was a young adult I moved to a different part of the country from where I had been raised. While there I regularly met women who were suppressing their intelligence, competence, and excellence for fear they might make a boyfriend or husband feel uncomfortable. In many cultures there is a sense that women "should not grow too much" lest they overshadow their husbands or cause them to feel threatened. I was struck in this research by how secure these women's husbands are, or how well they seemed to be managing feelings of insecurity if they arose. And I found myself pondering the fact that Jesus does not seem to be threatened by his bride.

For example, Megan said, "It's having a supportive spouse, even though I know that will sound hokey. It's still such an important thing. I can't tell you how many men have asked my husband, 'Doesn't it bother you that your wife has more education than you do?' He just looks at them and says, 'No. I'm confident in myself.'" Hannah's comments as a senior vice president reveal this as well:

> I think from the beginning, even before we began working in missions, we had a more mutual relationship. But if I had a husband who wasn't comfortable with what I do or who felt threatened in any way or felt challenged, there isn't any way I would put my marriage in danger to have a professional role. For me that has never been a consideration, but I've known women where it has been. I really feel for them. And they are not bad guys. A lot of them have just had a different upbringing or just do need a spouse who fills a different kind of a role. It doesn't mean they are weaker or not capable as husbands, but I've just always had it so easy because my husband—part of the reason he married me was because of my brain, and he was happy I could use it!

These women recognize the importance of having a supportive, non-threatened husband in their own journeys, and they see it as a significant hurdle for married women whose spouses do not have these traits.

I wonder if men feel threatened by their wives because they are competing with them. Since in many cultures men are taught to compete with other men, are they bringing this behavior into their marriages by default, without critically reflecting on why they should be responding differently? In Scripture we don't see Jesus in competition with his bride.

Does Jesus encourage his bride? As I grow older I am struck by how spouses sometimes treat one another. I think husbands and wives should speak well of one another; yet in many cultures it is common for husbands to verbally insult or embarrass their wives.[2] Perhaps it goes back to feeling threatened or insecure, but many husbands do not encourage their spouses when new opportunities arise. Again, I found myself thinking of Jesus with his bride. He encourages her! And so do the husbands of the women in this research. This chapter's epigraph relates what my husband said to me during a season when ministry responsibilities were especially heavy. Julia's story at the start of this chapter also illustrates this, and the importance of a husband's encouragement is prevalent in the other stories throughout this chapter.

Does Jesus want his bride to grow to her full potential? Throughout this research I was regularly struck by how husbands spurred the women on to take risks and grow beyond their perceptions of their own potential. As Katie said, "My husband is my greatest fan. He gives me responsibilities I do not believe I can handle, and he supports, coaches, and encourages me until I am able to do them." They work as a team in ministry (church planting). Some women spoke of husbands sharing with them resources, articles, and podcasts to encourage their leadership growth and development.

Gladys said her mother was a deeply gifted and trusted counselor in their tribal community, but her mother had no opportunity to get educated, so she remained illiterate throughout her life. Gladys said her mom was a great inspiration to her. Gladys was also influenced by her husband's ongoing encouragement to keep pursuing higher levels of education so she might be able to address different needs she was encountering. Now Gladys has a PhD.

As genocide was playing out in a neighboring country, Gladys was heartbroken. She saw United Nations groups and other aid groups doing what they could, but no one was training volunteers to help with the counseling needs people were facing. She said, "Each time I would come home to pour out my frustration to my husband: 'Why is no one realizing that the people are so traumatized with death, loss, grief and all that has happened?'" He listened patiently and finally asked, "Gladys, you keep asking what others are doing about trauma. What are *you* doing yourself?" She responded, "Me! What can I do? I am a woman, and a woman from Kenya at that. I don't have any money, and my counseling organization is small and unknown, and I've never even been to that nation!" She said with his usual patience he persisted, "I thought that you are a Christian before all those other things."

He was the catalyst that encouraged her to risk and train hundreds of lay trauma counselors to help people in that neighboring nation heal from the atrocities of genocide. Without her husband's honest questioning and critique, she would have never stepped into this new area and made the contribution in God's mission that she did. He has supported and helped her to grow in ways she never thought she could.

Does Jesus delight in his bride's accomplishments? Perhaps what struck me the most in my research is how much joy these husbands took in their spouse's accomplishments. It was as though they beamed with joy and pride as they watched their wives step into new and growing levels of leadership. It made me wonder if their responses mirror how Jesus delights when his bride wholly steps into her calling. For example, Leena said,

> My husband does not envy me. He would not want this role, the director role. Not the speaking engagements. None of that. He is also a very good supporter because he has this deep conviction and sense that God has called me. And so he is actually quite moved when he talks about it, because he just sees that this is how God is leading. How God is opening doors, and it's his role to be supportive of that. So I think that gives him joy. He even says when I travel and he is alone, "Well that's part of the sacrifice I put in, because we are together in this." So there is a sacrifice in following Jesus and being part of God's mission. There are treasures and joys, but there are sacrifices. One of them is that I am away at times.

Mama Maggie first felt a call to reach the poor in Egypt when she was young, but her father told her she needed to marry and pursue a typical path as a wife and mother. She obeyed his directions and married Ibrahim, a successful Egyptian businessman. However, after a number of years the calling she felt from the Lord only intensified. She left her successful career in business and teaching at the leading university in her nation to reach the vulnerable thousands living in Egypt's garbage dumps. Ibrahim stood with her and supported her efforts. From the proceeds of his business, he bought the first building she used to help children. Of his wife he said, "She is a sweet angel with an iron will and an ability to make miracles." Over time he came alongside her, helping her to see the vision that God put in her heart become a reality. "Eventually it became his full-time livelihood—a job he enjoyed much more than his profitable business, which he eventually sold to spend more time helping Mamma Maggie."[3] Ibrahim delights in seeing her realize her dreams, and he beams with joy that she has been nominated for a Nobel Peace Prize because of her efforts.

Reflecting on New Types of Questions

These are some of the questions I have pondered since doing the research. Over the years the primary message I have heard about modeling this mystery in marriage focused on the need for wives to *submit* to their husbands. We need to expand the scope of the questions we ask about what it means to model the relationship between Christ and his bride in our marriages, for the answers to these questions will determine whether or not many women will be able to fully develop and make their greatest contribution in God's mission around the globe.

Discussion Questions

1. What do you need to do your best work?

2. In what ways are you helping others to do their best work?

3. How do you see the mystery of Christ's relationship with his bride, the church, modeled in marriages in your work or ministry contexts?

4. Which aspects of how Jesus treats his bride do you think are easiest for people in your context to model, and which are more difficult?

CHAPTER TWELVE

A HEALTHIER METAPHOR
IN THE WORKPLACE

*As a celibate single woman, there are many assumptions made
about who I am and what I'm about, everything from being
homosexual to being a woman who is promiscuous and seeking
to have relationships with the married men in the organization.
Somehow I have been made to feel that I am responsible for the
sexuality of all the people with whom I have contact.*

MELISSA IS NORTH AMERICAN AND HAS LED
A MINISTRY THAT MOBILIZES PROFESSIONALS
IN HER FIELD TO SERVE IN MISSION
LOCALLY AND AROUND THE GLOBE[1]

*B*efore working in global mission, Amy led a thriving young adults'
ministry at her church. When she returned on furlough to visit
the congregation, she met the new young adults' pastor hired to take
her place. He was about ten years younger than Amy. As he shared
some of the difficult challenges he was facing in the ministry, Amy
said, "We ought to meet for coffee and talk." She said this because
she cared so much about the young adults in the group, and she
sensed she might be able to help him find ways through some of
the challenges he was facing. She had encountered some similar
hurdles when she began the position years earlier, and she thought

it might help if he didn't have to relearn all the same lessons the hard way by making the same mistakes. If they could talk things through, it might save him months or years of frustration and enable him to experience greater fruitfulness in the ministry.

However, the young male pastor responded, "Oh, I never meet a woman for coffee. If you want to make an appointment to visit with me at a time when my administrator is in the office, I would be willing to talk with you. Why don't you call her to schedule a time?" Amy was stunned. As she drove away from the encounter, tears began falling down her cheeks. She was single and already regularly feeling the sting of what many considered to be her socially deficient marital status. And now this new pastor somehow viewed her as a potential temptress who might lead him astray simply because of her gender? She never called to set up an appointment to meet with him, and within a short time he stepped away from leading the ministry out of frustration.

Explicit and Implicit Messages

Many women leading in mission locally and abroad struggle with what Amy experienced. Women are often left out of a wide variety of formal and informal settings open to men because people believe their gender predisposes them to "cause men to stumble." Yet it is often in these types of settings that coaching happens, new leaders are mentored, and fresh ideas and opportunities for ministry emerge. People get to know and trust one another better in these situations, and that foundation often leads to growth and pathways into new leadership roles.

Sometimes regulations regarding male-female meetings are explicit in ministry policies, which state things such as female colleagues can never travel with male colleagues, a male colleague can never be alone in an office with a female colleague, a male colleague cannot go out for coffee with a colleague of the opposite sex, and so on. Other times the messages are implicit yet equally potent. This happens in situations where leaders are only willing to mentor men, or when male leaders spend disproportionate amounts of time talking with male colleagues about work-related or personal topics, and time spent with female colleagues is kept to a bare minimum. Thus, women leaders are put in difficult situations if they desire to work late at the office, if they want fellowship and desire to discuss ministry as they travel to conferences and global meetings, or if they simply want to be able to get to know their colleagues better.

Take Responsibility for Your Own Issues

Ever since "Eve's sin" in the garden, it can feel like women are blamed for many of men's shortcomings and character defects (Genesis 3:12), especially in the area of sexuality. While there are women who choose a life of sexual promiscuity, in all my years of ministry I have not met any women leading in God's mission who had the intent of snaring a man and hoping to lead him down a destructive sexual path.

I believe in exercising wisdom when it comes to sexual sin and temptation, just as I adhere to wisdom when establishing processes in other areas (e.g., how money is handled).[2] It is wise to implement basic principles in a wide array of situations because we do not always know what sins people are struggling with. However, when implementing processes, care needs to be taken to ensure that women are not marginalized because some men have difficulty managing their sexual impulses. The real battle for men is disciplining their thoughts. If they focus on that process rather than spending time nurturing sexual fantasies (Romans 12:1-2), their normal responses will be to live faithfully regardless of whether or not a woman is present.[3]

Allison is involved in leadership development of women in her church-planting mission, and she and her colleagues are serving in various parts of the Muslim world. She said,

> Part of it is you have married men and single women in leadership and they never eat together, or the men go out for lunch and they are talking about team issues and leadership and vision, and they don't take the single women or even the married women. Then women don't get to participate setting vision and things like that.
>
> For years people have tried the "Let's just not be alone with the single woman," but that doesn't really work when you look at leadership positions in missions. There is moral failure even with people who espouse that view. So there's got to be an inner transformation. I really think for women's voices to be heard, there needs to be a way to talk together, relate together, love each other well and model that kind of community.

At that point Allison mentioned that she is wrestling with a new metaphor she believes might have the capacity to greatly help her organization. I believe it is incredibly helpful for women called to lead in God's mission.

Living into Our Eternal Calling as Sacred Siblings

Human beings are sinful. However, Christ died to atone for sin and make a way for us to be reconciled and restored in our relationship with God so we might be able to have lives set apart for him and his purposes. That is integral to the amazing gospel we proclaim through our ministries. John 1:11-13 gets at the heart of this: Jesus "came to that which was his own, but his own did not receive him. Yet to all who did receive him, to those who believed in his name, he gave the right to become children of God—children born not of natural descent, nor of human decision or a husband's will, but born of God."

The apostle Paul preached,

> Those who are led by the Spirit of God are the children of God. The Spirit you received does not make you slaves, so that you live in fear again; rather, the Spirit you received brought about your adoption to sonship. And by him we cry, *"Abba,* Father." The Spirit himself testifies with our spirit that we are God's children. Now if we are children, then we are heirs—heirs of God and co-heirs with Christ, if indeed we share in his sufferings in order that we may also share in his glory. (Romans 8:14-17)

The passage goes on in verse 19 to talk about how the world longs "for the children of God to be revealed." Philippians 2:14-15 talks of doing "everything without grumbling or arguing, so that you may become blameless and pure, 'children of God without fault,'" so that we might appear as lights in the world.

The term that has captured my heart and imagination as a healthy metaphor for the mission workplace is "sacred siblings." It comes from a book titled *Mixed Ministry: Working Together as Brothers and Sisters in an Oversexed Society.*[4] I love this term because it presents a vision that can help us imagine new ways of working together without explicitly or implicitly sending messages to women that they are temptresses or stumbling blocks. This image should be integrated in our daily prayers as we ask that God's "will be done, on earth as it is in heaven" (Matthew 6:10).

I have four brothers, and though my friends might have thought they were handsome or were attracted to them, I never saw my brothers that way. They were just my brothers. And even among those who are married, the percentage of the time spent in sexual activity is quite small. The overwhelming majority of time in a marriage is spent simply enjoying life together, talking together after a long day, encouraging one another, working together to help other family members, and so on.

If sexual activity comprises only a small part of marriage, why are we allowing concerns about sex to overshadow our work environments? Shouldn't we create structures that will reveal to the world the beauty of God's sons and daughters as they grow together in Christlikeness? The author of 1 John 3:1-3 writes,

> See what great love the Father has lavished on us, that we should be called children of God! And that is what we are! The reason the world does not know us is that it did not know him. Dear friends, now we are children of God, and what we will be has not yet been made known. But we know that when Christ appears, we shall be like him, for we shall see him as he is. All who have this hope in him purify themselves, just as he is pure.

We are sons and daughters of the living God. We all share the same heavenly Father. Jesus is our older brother, the one with the final authority who calls the shots about what is and is not acceptable.

We are all given the Holy Spirit that we might grow and be transformed to look like God's kids. Surely, "sacred siblings" is a healthier metaphor that should be shaping our policies and processes as we work together in God's mission.

Discussion Questions

1. What do you find most intriguing about the idea of being a child of God?

2. What types of policies does your employer or ministry have in place regarding men and women working together?

3. What implicit messages do these policies convey to women and men in the workplace?

4. What implications would the metaphor "sacred siblings" have for your work or ministry context?

CHAPTER THIRTEEN

MEN COURAGEOUSLY
OPENING OPPORTUNITIES

When you know women have something to say or to contribute
in a meeting where the majority are male, give them a platform
and be their advocate. Don't be threatened by gifted women. Their
giftedness comes from God, just as your giftedness comes from God.

NATALIA IS NORTH AMERICAN AND HAS SERVED AS
A MISSIONARY IN A RESTRICTED-ACCESS NATION
DOING PIONEERING WORK AND STARTING
A VARIETY OF MINISTRIES[1]

J iang-Li didn't envision herself as the leader of a ministry. When the ministry founder first talked to her about taking over, she was hesitant. However, she wanted to see a new paradigm implemented when media is used for evangelism and discipleship, and God put on her heart that she needed to lead for that vision to become a reality. Speaking of her situation, she said,

> There is definitely a majority of men. And it probably has something to do with the general patriarchal structure and then a little bit to do with how much this is a technology-dependent ministry. So I don't know if men just have more access. It's also got to do with the church structure, because we're working with existing ministries, and often they are

nominated pastors, or they are putting it out there to someone who has a seminary background. Actually, there are a lot of women in seminary, but they don't necessarily go on as pastors. I think they end up doing things like youth ministry and Sunday school.

When James asked me to take on this role, I was a bit concerned because, in terms of power points, I'm very low on them. I'm an Asian, a female, and I'm young. I'm not the classic—well, I'm not James—white, a pastor, large, and male.

But actually I haven't found many issues, and I think it actually has to do with the area where I'm working in, and the level of expertise. So something about the expertise I can bring trumps that I am female and younger, and so on. And one of the things that I think helps a lot is that I've had James standing very solidly behind me. So even though he hasn't been able to return to Asia, he has made it very clear that I am speaking on his behalf. So, that has covered a lot as well.

Jiang-Li was in her late twenties when she stepped into this role, and the ministry has tripled in size under her leadership.

Women Face Different Pressures

A consistent theme that arose in my research is the need for men to courageously open opportunities for women. Often women face social pressures that cause them to be unable to advocate for themselves. At other times a few influential and loud voices send messages throughout the body of Christ that hurt many women who God is inviting to serve and lead in his mission. Women know many men do not agree with those messages, but often women do not see men standing up and voicing different opinions. However, when they do, it can make a significant impact. There is a sense that many doors will never open unless men courageously take the initiative to make it happen and are truly committed to seeing change.

Women sometimes need men to open doors for them because of spoken and unspoken social pressures that work against them stepping into new roles. Even though in many parts of Europe women have a great deal of equality, Leena explained the tension many women in ministry face in her nation:

> I'm not saying there is a glass ceiling, but there is something there that makes it easier for young men to rise to leadership positions. I also think that men tend to be better at just aiming at those roles, applying for the positions, volunteering somehow. Women tend to hold back, waiting to be nominated, or to be asked. I can't give you any figures for this, but this is my personal observation.

While men are socialized to aggressively seek leadership roles, there are many subtle messages that such a focus is inappropriate for women, especially godly women.

Accusations and the associated fallout frequently occur when women try to open new doors for themselves. Beth, a North American, mentioned that in a former ministry environment, "Women weren't even asking to be ordained. They just wanted a voice. But everything that was suggested was voted down. It almost became more restrictive." In that ministry context, women were being penalized for voicing a desire for even a small measure of equality. Isabella expressed it this way,

> I think in my context in Latin America it's very important for other men to talk about women in leadership. But when

you as a woman start to talk about women in leadership, people say, "Oh, you are a feminist. Oh, you don't like the men." Many stupid things! But ... when men teach about this, they can learn. And obviously women need to be good leaders. But the men have the power. With that power they can open the doors for us.

Another young woman explained the situation in her ministry context: "I think the hard thing is these shifts wouldn't take place if you didn't have men who were willing to be that beacon for it. Any woman who would try to say, 'Hey, there are not enough women involved,' I think you still get the label 'feminist,' and you're kind of written off."

A Few Voices Eclipse the Broader Dialogue

Women face challenges at local, regional, and global levels when a small number of influential men argue that women should not be allowed to lead because of their gender. When this happens, if other men do not step in and voice their opinions, women are shut out of serving and leading in ways that further God's mission in the world. Yet women are able to flourish when men are willing to courageously speak up and support them. For example, Alia recounted her experience when she became the country leader for her mission agency:

You had some people from a very traditional background who would attack me. They would say, "Now, if you are the new leader, I will not support this mission anymore." So you felt terrible, like you are hindering or preventing your own members from getting their support. It was, in a way, a blackmailing situation. My male colleagues really helped me in that situation. They said, "No way will we let that happen. We wanted to have you here. And even if they stop supporting the mission, God will bring other people." So it was a few very traditional people who didn't want me here.

The influence of the few was so great, this leader was considering stepping down because of their loud voices. The support of her male colleagues enabled her to remain and serve for years as an exceptional executive director in her mission organization.

Sometimes the loud voices come from a specific seminary or Bible college in a nation or continent. When a few influential spiritual leaders teach that women should not lead in ministry, many women determine they must not have heard God correctly. Thus, they decide to not go into missions or ministry because the vision or calling God placed in their hearts does not fit those gender roles and stereotypes. Other times, because of globalization, the message that women are not supposed to lead comes from a famous pastor in another part of the world. It is hard to capture the depth of discouragement and sorrow this creates for gifted women called to lead in God's mission. These women might have led for decades and pioneered all kinds of new ministries and churches, yet because of a podcast of someone's teaching in another part of the world they are suddenly told they can no longer lead because they are female. Many thought the situation would be better when they got older only to find the divisive rhetoric around the topic is now worse than when they were young. Several older, gifted women leaders in my research expressed this concern. Jacqueline's sentiment captured what many told me, "I actually think after thirty-five years in ministry, the space for women is shrinking." Her context is North America.

Examples of the Power of Male Advocacy

A courageous male voice can have an amazing effect in these situations. Amelia is from the Pacific and has gone on to serve and lead in amazing ways in some of the most difficult parts of the world. One of these courageous male voices gave her the courage to step out and follow God's leading. She said, "One of my lecturers influenced me significantly. In that conservative pool, he was someone who has this amazing brain, who loves Jesus, and who didn't think the same way as everyone else. He wrote a paper about godliness and giftedness, and not gender, and that had quite an impact on me." Before hearing this professor's opinion, she was starting to question whether she should go into missions because of her gender.

Ellie explained how courageous men believed in her as she stepped out of a physically abusive marriage and was discerning God's call on her life. She said, "What a gift. So that was God's people, the church, supporting me in that extraordinary way." They helped her find herself in God's story, and that gave her a solid place to stand. Now she helps at-risk women and girls in the Middle East who are being trafficked and abused.

Victoria has been a significant leader in missiological circles. She spoke of the courageous path a respected male colleague followed by bringing to the attention of their academic society the need for female leadership. Before this, it had been male dominated. This man regularly integrated the topic into leadership conversations with the team and exercised care in selecting plenary speakers who would also encourage women leaders. There were times when he would be asked to speak at a conference, and he said he would only come if they also invited Victoria because he would say, "She is actually more of an expert than I am. She would be better."

Regarding leadership, Semira, an Ethiopian, said, "Of course the first thing is a woman's own character, performance, values, and skills and talents, education—all that. Their own development matters. Definitely." But then she said,

> One other thing I'm seeing, they need a male advocate who is in a position to do the advocacy. Like now, my colleague, my immediate supervisor, is very much supportive of my leadership. I've been traveling for almost a month. I've been traveling attending meetings. He has been supportive. If he wasn't, I don't think I would be able to do this. So, having a male advocate is especially helpful. We need those people who will stand in the gap.

This male colleague's support is making it possible for Semira to make contributions in all kinds of global initiatives. She said, I think women leaders "need a male figure who can stand for her. I don't think that revolutionary type, that Marxist type of movement to release women for leadership, will work. I don't think so. It just creates more resistance and conflict." She believes change will only happen through male advocacy.

Intentionality Is Essential

As so often is the case, courageously opening doors for women usually does not happen without intentionality and commitment. Wendy said it is easy for current decision-makers to think "the issue of women is still not high on our list of priorities." However, she continued,

The challenges today's leaders are facing are enormous, and so the issues of women don't tend to make it into the top priorities of what we have to deal with to be effective in the future. But I would suggest that if we prioritized our progress in integrating women, it would start speaking to most of the other issues we're grappling with. Funding—when women are engaged in that, we improve both in how we allocate resources and gain new donors. Recruiting, risk and safety, family issues, etc.—I think if we prioritize the dialogue on women and mission, it will give more creative thinking and more resources to all the challenges we are facing.[2]

Some women I spoke with observed that the growing edge of commitment and intentionality seems to be with the next generation. However, women need courageous men to speak up now or many opportunities for God's purposes to be advanced around the world will be lost as we wait for another generation to hopefully make their concerns a priority. If men do not advocate on the behalf of women now, large numbers of women will never be able to do their best work or make their best contribution in God's mission, and many around the world will suffer as a result. Without women's gifts of service and leadership, it is hard to fully fathom how many human beings around the world will never encounter the love of God and the good news of the gospel of Christ.

Discussion Questions

1. Have you ever had someone advocate for you when you needed help? If so, what was that experience like?

2. In what areas might different people need advocacy in your culture or workplace?

3. In what ways have you observed men specifically advocating for women in your culture or workplace?

4. What are one or two new ways men might be able to advocate for women in your culture or workplace that could have a significant impact for women?

CHAPTER FOURTEEN

CULTIVATING ENCOURAGEMENT AND GROWTH

Not just for women but for any leaders, I believe we need ac-
countability, someone to walk beside us, to accompany us, to
confront us when needed, to affirm us, and to remind us of our
flaws. Plus for crosscultural contexts, we need at least one
cultural guide. We need someone to tell us explicitly where or
how we are messing up, missing cues, and if we are making
mistakes as we speak or write the language.

LISA IS NORTH AMERICAN BUT HAS SPENT MOST OF
HER LIFE IN LATIN AMERICA LEADING AND TRAINING
LEADERS FOR A VARIETY OF CAMPING MINISTRIES[1]

Juliana, a Latina, told me, "Sometimes the higher up you get in leadership the less people think you need encouragement." She is such a gifted woman, and I think many who know her well marvel at how competent and talented she is. But she confided that she had recently turned in her resignation. Thankfully, her executive director did not accept it. She had labored intensely for a long time, and in the past twelve months she had navigated some of the mission's most difficult situations. As a woman leader, she was also carrying far more responsibility outside the workplace than many of her male counterparts. She had recently moved to a new country, and she had far fewer opportunities to be with her sisters, other close family members, and old friends. Over time she became deeply discouraged, questioning her own abilities and wondering if she had what it takes to be such a high profile leader. No one else would have questioned this, for all they were seeing was her talent, incredible instincts, and gifted strategic thinking. But inside she was withering because she was not receiving encouragement from people close to her.

Carrying the Weight of Leadership

As these women carry the weight of leadership, they need safe places where they can talk with others who care about them; people who can encourage them in difficult seasons that arise. They do not want to lead in isolation. They want to walk the journey with people, sharing life together and encouraging one another along the path. Whether single or married, with children or without, young or old, this issue was an ongoing reality in their lives. Some explained the joy of finding encouragement in adult children's compliments and praise as they watched their mom take on a public leadership persona. Others like Gladys mentioned finding support in her husband: "Since our marriage forty-four years ago my husband has been the wind in my wings, my prayer partner, my mentor, my encourager." Karen said, "I've had cancer twice, the death of a spouse, and currently I have guardianship of a four-year-old and a nine-year-old. For me it is very much community—having community, having close friends, having church community." The encouragement they receive through these relationships is a source of strength that gives them greater capacity to serve and lead in God's mission. For this reason it is important to know how to cultivate the encouragement they need to take risks and continue growing. One way to do this is by identifying what is harmful for their development and multiplying what is beneficial.

Discouragement Can Come from Other Women

It is easy to believe that the obstacles men place before women hinder women from fully growing and becoming the leaders God desires them to be. The mantra that "men are always the problem" is a common theme in many feminist movements. But that is not true. Several of the leaders in this research said other women posed some of the greatest obstacles they faced in ministry. As Isabella explained, "I've been discouraged to discover that many times the people who boycott us are other women, not men. It's other women. That was sad for me." Patricia said, "I have worked with some really great men, but there are also some times when woman to woman can be a challenge." The greatest resistance two of the women in the research faced came from their mothers—both of whom were married to pastors—yet they did not want their daughters moving away to serve God in mission. They wanted their grown daughters to marry, bear them grandchildren, and live nearby. In both instances, these normally godly mothers were impeding God's will, because it contradicted their expectations, desires, and stereotypes.

It is not uncommon that God calls women to serve and lead in ways they never expected or have never seen modeled by other women. A challenge they face is when other women in their lives hold harsh, judgmental attitudes about them choosing these different paths. Kristen's journey, for example, has taken many unexpected turns. She has been a homeschooling mom, a pastor's wife, and an executive director. She keeps a treasured family spinning wheel in her home as a reminder of prior generations. She said, "They cared too about their families and their homes," and she finds inspiration in that. But while she deeply values tradition, she also said, "Women should not judge one another. There is not one best or one right way. There are seasons, and God asks us to do all kinds of different things in different seasons of life. We need to give each other grace for these changes and not be threatened when others make different choices than us."

The harsh judgment women can thrust on one another can be intense and overwhelming. Depending on the setting, it ranges from "not being fashionable enough" to being "too fashionable," being judged "too talkative" as you try to get to know people, to being judged as "too aloof" when your approach is to listen carefully before talking, and so on. Of the complexity, Megan said,

> Then you add the cross-cultural piece that makes it even harder, because you want so much to not offend. The first international training event I went to, the fact that I have a PhD was respected, so that really helped. But a woman asked me, "How old are you, and how many children do you have? If you don't answer this question right, I'm not going to listen to you." And I was able to say that I was older than she thought and that I had three children. Then we were able to talk.

Hannah explained, "I think we need to give a lot of grace. And, yes, while we think we might have it figured out the way God intended it, everybody is not there, and everybody is not in the same place. And I think we need to have sensitivity toward that, while always making opportunities available to men and women. It's the whole thing of giving grace."

As I have watched so many different situations in various countries around the world, I've wondered if it is simply human nature to feel threatened when we see people assuming roles and living differently than we do. In my own journey, if things had gone other ways, I would hold very different views about women in leadership than I do now. The fact that I married later in life exposed me to ministries I would have never encountered if I had married in my late teens and had as many children as I dreamed and prayed would happen. If I had not experienced a series of miscarriages later in life when I did marry, I don't think I would have pursued a PhD. That different path led me to becoming a researcher, author, conference speaker, ministry consultant, and board member.

Seeing how God has used others and myself in these roles to help many people has changed what I believe regarding what is and isn't appropriate for women to do in mission. God often calls women to walk in a variety of paths they never anticipated, and it makes a big difference if other women in their lives can accept and encourage them when they take these leaps of faith to follow their Lord wherever he might be calling. A different choice or calling is often simply that, a different choice or calling, and not a judgment that other paths and other callings are less valuable or less significant.

Why Dialogue Needs to Be Understood

Many of the women I interviewed mentioned the need for genuine dialogue with men in various ministry contexts; however, I have witnessed over the years that men frequently converse differently from many women I know. Some gender differences seem to be highlighted in linguistic research as well.[2] For example, many men seem to enjoy debating. In these instances it becomes a power game with the goal of proving a position or winning an argument, regardless of whether or not the other person wants to argue.

I experienced this recently with an old friend as I was writing this book. He made many assumptions and leaps about what the book was going to be about and why I was wrong to not hold his opinions about what is and is not permissible for women to do in ministry. He sent an email afterward saying how energized he was by the conversation, yet I barely slept for the next two nights because I felt traumatized by it. As I watch men talk among themselves, at times I've seen dialogue being used as a form of competition, a type of one-upmanship, as a way of jockeying among themselves for power or status. Some women do the same in social settings, such as tiger moms comparing their children's accomplishments or status-conscious women wanting to prove their worth by talking about what they own or who they know.

However, this is not usually the way women serving and leading in God's mission like to converse. The women in this book mentioned a desire and need for a different form of conversation. They seemed to yearn for genuine dialogue: a place of discovery, learning, and a greater depth of understanding. They don't assume their experience in ministry is the same as someone else's. True conversation starts by setting aside assumptions about what you think women are experiencing, and instead taking time to actually talk with them. Many felt a strong need to be able to have honest dialogue about how to make sense of differing gender views regarding women in ministry leadership. For example, Rose spoke of mobilization ministry and said, "It seems like many women who feel called to this operate in something of a twilight zone. They want to have influence but seldom have an empowered role or platform from which to operate. There's a breakdown here that should be discussed and seldom is."

The different ways women talk and engage in dialogue are important to understand. For example, Magdalena, a Balkan leader, explained that men need to set aside more time to talk with women leaders than with male leaders, because women often communicate with fuller explanations and offer more extensive answers to questions. Many do not share bare facts alone but more of the nuances surrounding a situation or issue. Women in my research said things like, "We see and feel things differently. This is God's gift to you." Giving advice, Marie said, "I would say to the men, women are made differently from you. They see other areas that you might be blind to, so work with them. Ask questions to understand." She explained that sometimes women are more intuitive and might not be able to explain all the logical steps they followed to arrive at their conclusion, yet their ideas might be better and more fruitful in ministry. Women's ideas should not be discounted if they cannot explain their process in a way that mirrors how men might come to their conclusions.

I thought her comment was helpful because we are at the front end of a lot of neuroscience research that is showing the validity of intuition in problem solving. It is important to respect different ways of discerning God's leading, for in Scripture we often see God speaking in many different ways to people. Aesha said, "Women need to feel valued for who they are. Relationship is very important to them. Take time to relate to women as individuals, getting to know them and listening to them will help them flourish." I wholly agree because frequently genuine dialogue unlocks chains that keep women from making their best contributions in God's mission.

Prioritizing Diverse Forms of Mentorship

In almost every interview and survey, women stressed the importance of having mentors; however, gender issues can make mentorship more complicated. Also globalization is causing diverse people to work with one another in multicultural teams and contexts, so frequently former structures of mentorship no longer fit. If the only option for women leaders is to be mentored by another women, this leaves many in a precarious situation. As Jacqueline described doing pioneering campus work as a single, she said when the wife of her male staff member became ill, "I was on my own." Women should not be on their own, having to figure out leadership in God's mission by themselves.

Men mentoring women. When God calls women to serve in new types of leadership roles, being mentored is essential for them to be able to develop to their full potential and navigate the variety of pitfalls that can undermine their leadership and fruitfulness. Several women said they appreciated the mentorship they received from gifted male leaders. Talented male leaders influenced how these women conduct ministry, and many said their mentors' advice and examples over the years are why they are effective as leaders in their own ministry contexts. Often men mentored them because there were no women leaders in higher roles to facilitate that type of leadership development.

However, several others mentioned being told at times in their journeys when they requested to have a mentor that "men cannot mentor women." It goes back again to the image that the woman will somehow lead the man astray; she will "cause him to stumble." As Megan said, "I had tried for years to try to find someone who was willing to be a real mentor . . . that official relationship. The answer from the men was always no. 'I can't mentor a woman.'" It is terribly demeaning and frustrating when this happens, because often there are not yet women leaders in higher roles able to guide a new woman leader. Without mentorship new doors will likely not open, and there is a much higher chance that mistakes from the past will be repeated, and the organization as well as the leader will suffer as a result.

Women mentoring women. Women also bear the responsibility for mentoring new leaders, and some rise to the challenge while others do not. Adalie, a European, said, "When I started our mission organization I had so many questions. I wanted to get it all right, and I often had no clue. I wanted to have people journey with me." She asked many women to mentor her, but none would. She observed,

> Once I got through the rough times, into my sixth and seventh year, I had several guys journeying with me, investing into me, mentoring/coaching for various things like leadership, my soul as the leader.... But really I would have needed it back then when the task was so daunting and huge. I wish someone would have considered walking with me in leadership from the start, not when I already had a "name."

Adalie and others said when they asked women to mentor them, they were told the potential mentor did not have time to add this to her other responsibilities. This is understandable given that women are often juggling many additional responsibilities outside the workplace. However, a great opportunity is missed if they never mentor others.

Kristen said even a short time with one of her female mentors changed her life. She was considering a staff role in a nonprofit and her mentor told her she felt the role was beneath her abilities, and she should be looking into executive director positions. Kristen said she was stunned because she had never seen herself that way. It changed her whole professional trajectory even though the discussion was very short. She now tries to be an encouraging mentor for staff who report to her. Victoria is a young leader who also mentors others because of the help her mentors have been in her own journey. She said, "I've tried to make it the same policy that people did for me. I'll bring you along. I'll pull you into it."

Mentoring communities. Most people think of mentoring as a one-to-one relationship, but that is not the only option, nor is it always the best option. I believe mentoring communities can be a helpful way to sort through the gender tensions and concerns. If carefully designed, they can help both men and women grow to their full potential. Sharon Daloz Parks writes of the importance of mentoring communities for young adults.[3] However, I believe the concept is helpful at many stages of life. She writes that a personal mentor is what we need if we are going to enter a profession or organization "as it is presently defined."[4] However, if a person wants to help their profession, organization, corporation, or society develop in new and creative ways, "only a mentoring community will do."[5]

These communities provide networks of belonging that provide physical, emotional, intellectual, and spiritual support in tangible ways.[6] Mentoring communities might last for brief periods of time, or they may extend for years. Despite how long they last, they can be extremely influential.[7] The features of mentoring communities include networks of belonging; big enough questions; encounters with people different from ourselves; growing in habits such as dialogue, reflection, and critical thinking; and envisioning the future.[8]

Encounters with diverse types of people provide transformative moments of perspective-taking and opportunities for examining deeply held but often tacit assumptions. They are places where people listen, seek to understand, and are willing to be affected and change their minds.[9] In essence they are living examples of humans sharpening one another (Proverbs 27:17). They provide safe places to "reach for the ideal" and begin to imagine how life might be.[10]

Women like Havilah and Semira have found these types of mixed-gendered communities outside of their ministry workplaces in other networks and ministries. Often these can become places of tremendous growth and stretching, and the female leader is then able to bring this back into her own ministry context. Others like Angelika and Elspeth have formed them with other women who they journey with as a group. Over the years their trust has deepened and they have grown in their ability to learn from and challenge one another. Joyce still carries the advice from a church that years earlier provided this mentoring foundation for her. She explains what it was like when God opened up a leadership role for her in the area of itinerant preaching:

> One of the gifts of the local church where I landed was two of the pastors who I'm still friends with now. One was the national pastor for the denomination. He said, "We are just going to let you be a person in this congregation. We see your gifts are very unique, and it would be really easy to ride the coattails of what God has given you to grow our church. But we feel you've been treated a little like a commodity and not a person. So in our local context you just get to be a person."
>
> So I never preached there for three years. I was just a person. Very few people knew that I was an itinerant preacher. They

had two main requirements for me. They didn't require it, but they said if you want our input pastorally—never travel alone, and be in a small group or a Sunday gathering twice a month.

I thought, *No one is going to pay for two airfares!* Right? It's hard enough to believe someone is going to ask me to preach. But they are not going to pay for two of us? They just said, "We think it is best. There are people who get on that itinerate circuit, and they get that stage persona, and no one knows if this story is true or not true. Pride creeps in, and they think of themselves more highly than they should. And then loneliness can get in there and isolation, and you can be more vulnerable to sexual sin." They just had some real wisdom.

Her mentors in that community recommended that she bring someone with her whenever she traveled, and Joyce marveled at how, eighteen years later, no one ever said no to paying for two airfares. Following their advice has provided a chance for her to bring friends, prayer partners, people she is discipling, other church leaders, and sometimes her husband now that she is married. She said, "I never have difficulty finding someone to come. They like to learn in that context. It provides a different kind of safety, belonging, so I don't have to navigate those things on my own."

Another missionary talked about going overseas in her professional role but relying on a missionary mentoring community to help equip her and her husband for what they would face when they reached that nation. She did not have colleagues or friends who could mentor her, but this other community was able to provide that type of support. Therefore, learning communities can take different shapes and forms.

A Bonsai or an Oak Tree?

There are so many reasons to make excuses to not mentor people. It seems like life is simply getting busier by the day. Time can be in such short supply that it is difficult to see how to add one more thing to the list of responsibilities we are already carrying. In other situations it can feel like the person who wants to be mentored is expecting you to be a sage or guru, and you simply don't see yourself that way. I have faced that scenario in the past, and I tell young leaders I am willing to mentor them in some ways if they will mentor me in others (e.g., technology or helping me to understand their generation better). So mentoring varies greatly depending on culture, context, personalities, and purpose. But if we want women to fully grow into all God is calling them to be, and not be stunted or dwarfed in their development, encouraging and mentoring them has to be a top priority.[11]

Discussion Questions

1. What enables you to stay encouraged in your work or mission context? Do you encourage people in your work or ministry context? Why or why not?

2. In what ways do you see women encouraging or hindering others in your work or ministry contexts?

3. What are the dreams you have for yourself or others that you are most tempted to hold on to, rather than God's will and provision, believing they will ensure your future happiness, value, worth, or security?

4. How is mentoring done in your work or ministry context, and how might creative mentoring communities help to address some of the challenges you are seeing?

CHAPTER FIFTEEN

ADDRESSING
REMAINING ISSUES

*When you have the benefit of flextime, you find that when you
sit down to work, you give it so much quality, because something
in you tells you must give it your best. It was such an amazing
motivator for me to do my best. And the big piece is trust. Once
somebody is a leader, they are a leader. Unless they have given
you reason to doubt their self-governance, they should be OK.*

NICOLE IS FROM EAST AFRICA AND MENTORS
LEADERS AND ORGANIZATIONS IN
MANY PARTS OF THE CONTINENT[1]

*A*llison was born in North America, but she has spent much of
her life in church planting and outreach ministries in the
Muslim world. She spoke about how much she appreciated the
fact that her mission found ways to help her stay engaged in
the ministry at different seasons in her life. She explained that
while a male church planter might spend his extra time at a ministry office, it might be possible for the vast majority of a woman's
ministry to be done out of the home. She said, "I think it's probably
a little tougher for young married women with kids than it is for
young single women. I really appreciated our mission having flexible
ministry descriptions when my kids were little so I could minister

in my home and out of it." She believed that if supervisors accepted and encouraged flexibility, more women would stay engaged in God's mission through different life stages even when family responsibilities affected them in a variety of ways. She said that often, with a bit of creativity, new ways of doing ministry could emerge that might be more fruitful than what has been done in the past.

Flexibility Is Important

The women I interviewed said repeatedly that females in the ministry workplace need greater flexibility because they often carry heavier loads than their male colleagues. Many are expected to put their professional responsibilities on hold when family needs arise. In addition, women often have to wrestle with diverse health issues, and sometimes as they talk about what they are experiencing misunderstandings arise with male colleagues. The following are a sample of the challenges women face, along with remaining issues that need to be addressed for women to stay engaged and do their best work in God's mission.

Life-stage obstacles. "Prayer, culture learning, and hospitality are things that we can do at any of our life stages, and they are very significant."[2] This is so true, yet life stages bring with them a variety of challenges for women in leadership. Women serving and leading in God's mission often need greater flexibility than their male counterparts to design their schedules and enable them to meet the various challenges and obligations that arise because of their gender. In each country, ministry and family circumstances can vary significantly. Whether single or married, they are often called on to help ailing parents, siblings, children, or other relatives.

Therefore, genuine dialogue with the women in your ministry workplace is the best avenue to ensure you have structures and policies in place that enable talented women to continue leading in ministry.

Needs of single women. A variety of issues impact singles, but one that is rarely mentioned is the assumption that because a woman is single, she will be assigned to live with another single woman in their ministry location. However, serious incompatibility issues can surface in these living arrangements, which can make being at home a horrid and draining experience. As one leader said, "You are stuck living with whoever they put you with, unless it's your own husband." If single women are expected to focus and do their best work in mission, they need flexibility in choosing their living arrangements.

Needs of married women. Marriage makes some things easier and others more complex. For example, when I was a single leader, I traveled frequently. It was hard coming home to find that my friends were traveling, because they were my support system. But as a whole, I had tremendous flexibility to go almost anywhere. Once I married, I had a much more consistent support system, but I felt it wasn't fair to my husband if I was traveling all the time. Thankfully, my organization understood my concern and the trips decreased in frequency. I have noticed, however, that the wives of many men I work with provide them with a great deal of personal and professional support. Sometimes they accomplish a lot of their husband's administrative responsibilities, oversee correspondence, or even pack their bags for upcoming trips. My husband could not do this because of his own demanding career. So, even though both male and female colleagues might be married, women in leadership often need more flexibility to carry out their duties.

Parenting responsibilities. Parenting responsibilities vary greatly depending on the age of children. Nicole is Kenyan, and she said it helped immensely when she was able to talk honestly with her boss after her baby was born. Normally, colleagues needed to arrive at the office by 8 a.m. While she had a nanny at home with her baby, she still needed to get up at 4 a.m. to ensure the nanny had enough breast milk to make it through the day while Nicole was at work. Of this season in life, she said, "Now I think one of the things that I struggled with the most through my time with my young children and my work was just wondering if I needed to quit. That was a very big piece. Every morning—every morning—was tearful. Every morning was, *What am I doing? How can I leave my children?*" Thankfully, her boss valued her contribution as a leader and asked what she needed in this new season. Once she explained the challenges she was facing, he gave her a shorter workday at the office and flextime to work from home.

The women interviewed were able to travel easily when their children were older, but it was important to have shorter trips when they were young. Other times they had flexibility to bring a baby to the office or to have childcare provided onsite so they could spend time with their children during breaks. Before international trips, Nydia would prepare all her family's meals in advance for a week, schedule all of the children's school and extracurricular events and transportation in advance, do all the laundry, and fully clean the house—all in addition to preparing professionally for the meetings and responsibilities she had as a leader. She needed flexibility before and after trips to juggle all of this. Others needed the chance to work remotely when they were back in their home countries getting young adult children settled into the next phases of their lives. Sometimes this was also needed at the birth of a grandchild if adult children did not have other forms of help during these transition seasons.

Caring for elderly parents. Caregiving was also a common theme in my research. Often these women are in some of their most influential leadership roles at the same time their own mothers and fathers are becoming elderly and frail. Andrea is incredibly gifted and respected by her peers in the medical missions community. Regarding caring for her elderly mother, she said, "I think again flexibility is key. I can work remotely, which helps a lot, and I can set my own hours if I have to go with my mom to a doctor's appointment. I personally don't think I would be more effective if I worked at the headquarters. Most of the people I work with are outside our headquarters, and a phone and computer is all I need." She continued, "I try to discern what travel I need to do for my job. In some cases I can have my associate director do it." Often a team approach makes it work well, and that approach can actually provide avenues for developing a larger group of leaders. In other instances, seasons of caregiving can be a time for starting new types of ministries, like blogs or new forms of communication, and these new ministries can enable women to lead in strategic ways even though their daily schedule in an office is not as consistent as it was before they needed to care for an elderly parent.

Other family needs. All kinds of other family needs arise as well, and often the family expects the daughter, sister, niece, mother, grand-mother, or granddaughter to put aside her professional responsibilities to carry the largest share of the load. Women in my research spoke of caring for aunts with Alzheimer's disease, adult siblings with disabilities, grown children with developmental disorders, various responsibilities with family businesses, and so forth. Each situation is unique and requires a different strategy.

Flexibility with Health Challenges

Many of the talented leaders included in this research mentioned challenging health issues. Sometimes these lasted for months, and other times they were ongoing chronic conditions. Often they needed understanding and flexibility from male colleagues as they navigated these issues. However, because of the nature of the problems they faced, some men were afraid to talk about women's health challenges, or they misunderstood when women addressed them so openly. Greater understanding about these issues can provide the support women need to navigate these issues in order to do their best work in God's mission.

Fighting our bodies again! Many women sense that they have been battling their bodies for as long as they can remember. Young girls' bodies change and morph in ways they cannot control. These changes often bring unwelcome attention from boys and men that we frequently do not want, and that sometimes put us in dangerous and abusive situations. As years passed, many of us wrestled with pregnancy or the inability to get pregnant. Both ends of that spectrum tend to bring intense emotions. And all the while we fought our bodies as they released or withheld hormones that deeply affected our moods, attention, alertness, memory, focus, and weight. As years pass, we have to face menopause and all the additional unpleasant side effects it creates, such as intense mood swings, hair loss, sleepless nights, and higher risk for all kinds of dangerous health issues.

I personally look at my kind husband and wonder what it must be like to wake up each day with consistent blood chemistry. His initial thoughts are not spent having to sort out why he feels blue or happy for no reason at all. It is astounding that many men experience consistency in their moods because their bodies are not fighting them all the time. For women, it can be a constant battle to keep our bodies from blocking our ability to respond in consistent and loving ways according to our best intentions and values.

Openness about challenges. One of the areas that can confuse men is how readily many women discuss personal health issues. Often from the time we were young girls, we were socialized to learn how to deal with health challenges by getting advice from peers who walked through similar challenges. From this socialization arise a number of traditions like wedding showers or baby showers, where all kinds of advice is shared. A variety of spontaneous conversations take place among friends, and sometimes absolute strangers in grocery stores, regarding pregnancy tips, side effects from female issues, navigating hormonal challenges, dealing with menopause, and the like. All of these conversations normalize what at times feels like a freakish experience happening within these bodies God has given us.

And if the ongoing normal challenges in daily life are not enough, because of our gender it seems we are subject in much larger percentages to all kinds of serious illnesses such as breast cancer, cervical cancer, and ovarian cancer. We struggle in disproportionate numbers with chronic issues such as fibromyalgia, rheumatoid arthritis, osteoporosis, and lupus. It gets so intense at times that talking about it with others becomes the most common way to learn how to manage the challenges. Reflecting on the challenges of navigating a chronic health issue that seemed to arise out of nowhere during menopause, Lauren observed, "There is so much value in being open about it with each other, listening to each other, and validating with each other what we are going through. I am very motivated to do that. That to me is what has helped me to cope with it."

Not all women want to talk about what they are facing. Some are extremely private about these matters. However, after working with many men over the years, I have personally witnessed that women speak of their health challenges far more readily in the workplace than most of their male peers. Yi-Ling, who struggled with breast cancer, said, "When the news of the cancer came, I think the first thought was, *Wow, death. That equates with death.*" She said she had "assurance of Jesus' love. That he doesn't do this because he hates me or doesn't love me, or because I did something wrong. He just loves me whatever I am, even if I lose body parts in surgery. He still loves me." She said she sent out a global request for prayer to colleagues "as a cry for help."

Misunderstandings. When this sharing happens in the workplace, men can unintentionally make the situation worse. Women share openly, as they have for decades, but in leadership roles they are working with more men than in the past. They talk openly, and some men back away, avoiding them and refusing to mention the medical challenge the woman colleague is facing. When this happens, women feel abandoned and alone.

Some men, though, respond in an opposite way. They rush in and try to fix things, assuming that lessening the woman's load will make it easier and better. However, many women interpret this as their male colleagues now doubting their ability to lead well. As a result, these women suffer even more deeply, now fighting not only their bodies but also feelings of being misunderstood or fears of no longer being trusted by colleagues.[3]

Genuine dialogue is needed in these situations. Each woman is different, and so is the seriousness of the health challenges she is facing, the amount of support she has in her personal life, how the health issues are affecting her job performance, and how long the challenge is likely to last. Rather than avoiding the health crisis or rushing in and making assumptions about what a woman needs, it is best to have honest and safe discussions with her when these circumstances arise. It is also helpful to not ask for decisions from her immediately regarding what would be most supportive, for many women need time to sort though the implications, especially if they recently received a serious diagnosis.

Weathering the storms. Frequently, even amid serious diagnoses, many women are able to pull through and continue to serve and lead in fruitful and effective ways. Some can do it without a break in service. Others might need time for surgery and medical treatment. But, as with so many of the challenges they have weathered over the years, often women are resilient and able to continue to devote themselves fully to what God is asking them to do. And when this happens, they become even greater leadership models for others who will likely have to weather similar storms in the years ahead.

Advice for Executive Teams and Boards

This book is filled with a great deal of information that can be helpful if executive teams and boards would like to see their ministries and organizations become more welcoming places for women leaders. However, what follows are a few additional ideas that might be worth considering.

1. Develop a task force or issue group to do research within your ministry to find out what women in your context are experiencing. Take care to ensure confidentiality and safe places where they can share their thoughts without fear of retribution or worry that others will lose face through the process. Often this means asking a different person who is trusted in the ministry to collect this information through dialogue.

2. Consider accessing and using tools being developed in the area of unconscious gender bias. For more information, Leanne Dzubinski at Biola University has been doing a great deal of research in this area.*

3. Take time to examine your policies and practices. Ask women within as well as outside of your organization to share with you how they perceive these. Change the policies and practices that are hindering women or are sending implicit messages that they are less welcome as leaders.

4. Network with ministries that have an excellent track record of developing gifted women leaders. Ask if their leaders will work with your team or recommend consultants who can help you make changes that are needed.

*See Jenna Loumagne, "Biola Professor Presents Research on Unconscious Gender Bias in the Workplace," Biola University, July 19, 2017, http://now.biola.edu/news/article/2017/jul/19 /biola-professor-presents-research-unconscious-gend.

Tackling Remaining Structural Issues

Though I have already raised many issues in previous chapters, it is important to be intentional about tackling some remaining structural issues that hinder women from making their best contribution in God's mission. What follows is a sample of additional areas to be considered based on this research. However, because each ministry context is different, honest feedback and dialogue are often the best ways to uncover the significant issues in your ministry context and how to prioritize which issues to tackle first.

Fair human resource policies. Human resource policies and processes send a myriad of implicit messages throughout a ministry. They guide the subtle and not so subtle ways "we do things around here." In these policies and processes, women experience messages that they are either seen and valued or invisible and unimportant.

Equitable job titles and job descriptions. One of the disturbing aspects of doing this research was seeing how invisible so many women are in mission organizations and ministries. The example of Bible women mentioned in the opening chapter reveals how this invisibility has been an ongoing issue for centuries. Women from specific countries or those fulfilling specific ministry roles are especially at risk of being lost in systems often designed to work for male personnel and male placement situations. Women somehow fade into the background, even though they are often doing exceptional and fruitful ministry. Allison shared an idea that her mission organization is undertaking to address this:

> One of the things that happened a few years ago that really helped was coming up with titles for women leaders on our teams rather than "team leader's wife"—*This is my team leader's*

wife. Why are we defining her role like that? Instead, we started coming up with a title that affirms and validates her role as a leader. So, I really appreciate that because it actually helps them to see their role in a serious way, and it also gives other people clarification—this person has a role to play and I can talk to her about issues. I think having titles, not that you do it for the title's sake, but you're not just the wife of somebody.

I found this to be especially true with pastors' wives. They often oversee ministries in ways that would be equivalent to what significant leaders do in other churches and ministries. However, since they are not paid or because they are a woman, all they do falls under the generic "pastor's wife" title. I wonder if much of the debate about what women can and cannot do in ministry would evaporate if each woman in ministry had an honest job title that captured her responsibilities regardless of whether or not she was paid for her service and leadership. So many women are given job titles such as "coordinator," "assistant," or "administrator" when a man with the same ministry responsibilities would have a different title.

Fixing the wage gap. This issue was mentioned a number of times in my research. Women should not be asked to do work as volunteers when men doing the same work in the same ministry context are getting paid for their service. And women doing the same work as men should receive equal pay if they have the same qualifications and are have the same responsibilities in the same organization or church context. This is a justice issue, but in many places it is not common practice.

Proportional development and promotion. Women have deep concerns about the disproportionate amount of funding put into developing men for leadership in comparison to women. Comparing the budget line items can be jarring to women in a ministry, because the discrepancy often sends a powerful message that they are not seen or valued.

Similar feelings arise when women fill leadership roles throughout the organization but only men are put in senior roles with status, good salaries, and benefit packages. Women are not often considered for these roles, yet they also have extensive leadership skills and experience. This can be demoralizing, especially given that so many women leading in God's mission now have high levels of education as well.

For example, Amelia said, "I'm very sure in the contexts where I've been, had I been a male I would have been mentored or tapped on the shoulder. A lot of my own walk has been—I've stumbled into it. So it's not so much how I've led but how others might have developed me as a leader." This was especially noticeable when Amelia compared what happened when she was a young adult. She went through seminary with a few other women and one guy, but the guy was developed for leadership. She ponders the situation now in her mission. She said they were looking for a new international director, and despite the mission's female roots, only men have ever held that position. She said, "It is a systemic problem we have that a female wasn't put forward as a leader."

Planning meetings and conferences. The lack of women in meetings or as plenary speakers at conferences is truly baffling, and I believe it is wrong given that so much of the global mission movement is composed of women. Elspeth commented,

I think [it's] both-and. I think organizations need to be intentionally aware around issues of diversity. Issues around diversity such as, Are we incorporating our Asian colleagues and African colleagues? Are we incorporating people with different personality types, and how will that work? And real awareness—watching when you invite people to an event—not counting and watching percentages but making sure the right people are there. Does that include making sure the right women are there? When you are identifying participants for an activity, who is deciding who it should be?

When male leaders are asked why there are no female plenary speakers or no women included on an important project, their answer often is, "We never thought about it." That is not acceptable when women are half of the population, more than half of the active members of congregations, and more than half of the global mission force. Given those statistical realities, saying women never crossed their mind is simply unfathomable, unless the reason is that they are not valued. As one of the women said, "Yes, I think it is the intentionality that needs to be there. You can't just sit around and wait for it to happen. But we need to be intentional. People need to be thinking about it."

Travel policies. Several of the women pondered the fact that men often represent their organizations at important meetings, and it is common that they travel in packs. Theresa observed, "Men tend to come to conferences with their friends. I haven't seen women doing that." I'm not sure if that is because there is more funding for men to go to conferences and bring other men they are mentoring, or if women are simply juggling so many other responsibilities that they do not have as many female colleagues with margin to attend these gatherings. Other times there are travel policies that men and women in the organization are not permitted to travel together because it might look bad or reflect poorly on their witness. When this policy is in place, men enjoy fellowship while the woman is often alone. As one of the women explained, "An international flight is a really good time to get to know people, and to talk about work things. But, with evangelical restrictions, you are likely on another flight or you travel alone." That type of isolation, she noted, can be quite difficult to navigate.

What women leaders need to flourish. When women are not integrated into discussions and decisions, it is assumed that when something works well for men, it will automatically work great for women too. An essential aspect that is frequently overlooked is the importance of educating male colleagues about what women need to flourish. This book is a step in that direction. Several women in my research spoke about their frustration that most men they know rarely read books about women or by women authors. One of the reasons so many gifted leaders got involved in this research is because this book is designed for both males and females. Numerous women stated how necessary this is; otherwise discussions about women serving and leading in God's mission are no more than "preaching to the choir."

A beneficial piece on communication in the workplace, written by Wendy Wilson, enables men to understand how to help women negotiate invitations regarding promotions and new opportunities.[4] For example, many women automatically reject promotions because they are concerned about juggling new and expanding leadership roles faithfully without harming other responsibilities they have both inside and outside the ministry. However, if they are given some time to consider the invitation, many return a few days later and say yes. They simply needed time to figure out how to address various ripple effects that would arise if they accepted an expanded leadership role. Understanding even a few simple things about how women respond to leadership invitations can help significantly in increasing female leadership within a ministry or organization.

Uprooting gender biases. Uprooting unconscious gender biases, often from our socialization during childhood, can be quite challenging. One of the difficulties women face in leadership is when they have a boss or executive director who thinks he is wholly fair to women yet still exhibits many gender biases without even being aware he is doing so. This is the nature and complexity of the phenomenon of unconscious gender bias. Experiencing this, Rachel said, "The problem is if I challenged him about it, it would be my problem, not his problem. Because he believes in equality, there is no space for him to grow under that rubric." Another said, "There are subtle (and not so subtle) prejudices by both men and women in Christian leadership. Although if they were asked, they would deny this because they are not even conscious of it. Unspoken, unrealized attitudes are the hardest to change."

These women leaders realize that in the overwhelming majority of cases, male colleagues do not intend to hurt them or to be biased. Their hearts are often in the right places, and the majority are unaware of how their speech and behaviors leave women feeling marginalized and sidelined. But women are frequently left with no way to address these situations as they arise because by doing so they will be labeled "difficult," or worse yet in evangelical circles many will label them as angry feminists. Research about unearthing unconscious gender bias is growing and worthy of attention.[5]

Get on with It

A colloquialism kept surfacing as I interviewed British women leading in God's mission. They often used the phrase "get on with it." It seems to mean, "Quit spending all kinds of time talking about a problem and get busy doing something about it." As I've reflected on this, I think it genuinely captures a broader sentiment of the women in this research. For years they have heard people talking about gender injustice and inequities. Women want and need to see ministry leaders "getting on with it" and genuinely addressing these issues.

Discussion Questions

1. What types of family situations are most likely to cause women to drop out of the workforce in your context? What types of creative approaches might enable them to continue making a strategic contribution during these seasons of their lives?

2. What do you find helpful when you face health crises or other obstacles you did not expect? Or what have you learned as you have observed women navigate health challenges?

3. What structural issues still need to be addressed in your workplace or ministry context for women to do their best work?

4. What might it look like to "get on with it" in addressing the structural issues you identified?

CONCLUSION

WHAT MIGHT THIS MEAN FOR THE FUTURE?

*T*his book represents many of the things I learned as I set aside time to stop and listen to talented women who are respected leaders in God's mission. They were born and raised in approximately thirty countries, and they are leading in many additional nations across the globe. The depth of their wisdom challenged and deeply enriched my life. I hope their insights have enriched your life as well. In the midst of this research, I regularly had a sense that we are at the earliest stages of this important conversation about what women need in order to do their best work in God's mission. What follows are a few final insights that might help to inform the ongoing dialogue.

Moving Beyond Polarized Views

I mentioned this earlier, but it bears repeating: the women I interviewed and surveyed do not want to fight, argue, or debate about what women can or cannot do in mission because of their gender. They don't want to waste their time and energy in that conversation. They had no control over whether they were born a little girl or a little boy. What they have control over is whether or not they will faithfully follow and obey the voice of their Lord and Savior (John 10:27).

I don't know why God was not more consistent and explicit in Scripture regarding women. I know some people see a black-and-white reality there, but I believe an honest examination shows that Jesus was regularly upending religious and cultural ideas about women. He entrusted them with ministry responsibilities that at best were regularly misunderstood by others and at other times were wholly resented.

Women don't know why God often asks us to do things that go against what other people, especially some men, think we should be doing. But because of this reality, we are stuck in the middle having to decide whether to follow a male leader's strong opinions regarding gender roles in mission or to honor the calling and beckoning of our Lord. It's an incredibly difficult situation to be in, and I'm deeply concerned that many men who rigidly teach about what women can and cannot do have little understanding or empathy regarding the level of distress they are creating for gifted women around the globe.

The polarized two-category theological system is profoundly inconsistent, and I do not believe it is serving the global church well in God's mission. As Allison said, "We need new language." And Natalia said, "What I would really like to see is less talk about are you complementarian or egalitarian, and having people be more in the middle without committing to one or the other. But just saying, 'Let's just do the Great Commission. And what are we doing as men and women to fulfill that?'" Carolyn Custis James, a respected North American author, aptly states, "No matter what view we take on debates over Christian womanhood, we want to know how to live faithfully as followers of Jesus Christ. We don't want to waste our lives."[1]

I personally think we need more work like what Michelle Lee-Barnwell did in her book *Neither Complementarian nor Egalitarian: A Kingdom Corrective to the Evangelical Gender Debate*. She moves readers past simplistic and polarized categories to broader theological questions. She focuses on the larger theological themes that should be driving these conversations, such as unity, inclusion, and multiple examples in Scripture of reversals in cultural understanding regarding power and authority.[2] This broader focus would better serve our Lord and his purposes in the world, given that God seems determined to use women in diverse ways in many different contexts around the globe. In one Asian country, for example, God used a revival among teenage girls to burst forth the gospel in that nation, and those little girls have grown up to be extraordinary church and mission leaders. God does not seem to be following the clear gender lines and boundaries that many leaders want to impose on women. Just as God's work in the life of Cornelius caused church leaders to rethink what was and was not permissible (Acts 10:1-48; 15:1-35), I believe that the way the Holy Spirit is working around the globe needs to cause us to rethink our simplistic black-and-white mandates about what is and is not permissible for women in his mission.

Moving Beyond the World's Definition of Success

The next issue I would like to address is the message many younger women are hearing. It is the idea that they must be successful, but success is defined by the values of their surrounding cultures. Men are most often socialized to believe that success means grasping for the highest positions in organizations. In my culture, when people get a promotion in their company or organization, they sometimes say, "I'm one step closer to 'being the man.'" They mean they are one step closer to the top of the organizational pyramid, where they can make final decisions and have the greatest amount of power, prestige, and resources. At times I worry young Christian women are buying into this false view of success, as though they have to somehow climb to the highest rung of a leadership ladder to have "achieved it all" or to be truly successful.

I had an interesting talk with an old friend of mine during my research. We were neighbors about twenty years ago when we lived and worked in Asia. At that time many of her colleagues asked if she would let her name stand to be considered for the position of country director for the mission, but she declined. However, she has gone on to do macrosocial-change ministry. Through her efforts, all kinds of vulnerable children and people have been helped through policy initiatives that have impacted millions of people. If she had the view being espoused by many today, she would have let her name stand because that position would have been seen as more successful. While she would have been great in that role, I think by choosing differently she has had a greater impact in the world.

I deeply appreciate Mama Maggie's perspective. The fruit of her work has also helped so many people, and she has been nominated multiple times for the Nobel Peace Prize. Yet, even amid all of those external accolades, she has not forgotten what is truly important:

> We don't choose where or when to be born. We don't choose where or when to die. But we can choose either to help others or turn away. We can choose to do nothing or be a hero. If you want to be a hero, do what God wants you to do. He

will let you know what that is, as long as you are open to finding out.[3]

Real success is not striving and grasping for power, prestige, or the highest rung on a ministerial or organizational ladder. Real success is obeying and following God on whatever unique path he might have for you. That may mean letting your name stand for the highest leadership position in an organization, or it might mean something quite different. In the end if we substitute following our culture's definition of success for following God's voice, I believe we will never reach our full potential or make the contribution the world so desperately needs.

What Will You Choose?

It is incredibly easy to place our own comfort or the desires of others before obeying and following God. However, as Gladys explained,

> To flourish in maturity and ministry, we as women need to remember that our first love is Jesus Christ. It is to him we owe all loyalty. It is him who saved us and called us individually to himself, not through fathers, husbands, or children. God does not have grandkids such that the faith or ministry of a father or husband replaces his direct demand on our lives.

Are we willing to let God have his way in our lives and in the lives of women we know and love as well? As Chin-Sun said, "It is true that due to Korean culture and ministry context, women are kept from serving in many areas for the kingdom of God. Because of this limit, I think, women can be regarded as the huge potential resource in the kingdom of God." If this potential goes unrealized, however, not only women will suffer.

Perhaps revisiting a quote mentioned at the start of this book is also a good way to end it. Surely, "the full flourishing of God's sons requires and even depends on the full flourishing of his daughters."[4] We all suffer if women do not faithfully follow God in his mission and develop to their God-given potential.

What will you choose to do with what you have learned through this book? Will you choose to entrust your life to God and faithfully follow him? Will you hinder or help to expand the influence of faithful women in a world that so desperately needs their contribution? These are sobering choices we have to make.

Through God's mercy and kindness may we choose wisely!

ACKNOWLEDGMENTS

Normally authors take this moment to highlight the names of all the people who helped and supported them. However, many of the gifted women who helped me with this project can never have their names mentioned, for it will put their ministries and their colleagues at risk.[1] As a way to stand in solidarity with them, I will forgo mentioning specific names at this time. Instead, I want to thank each person who helped with this book. If it turns out to be a blessing in the world, it is because of you and the amazing contribution you made.

I also know you are exceptional as you serve and lead in God's mission because of the kindness and support of others. They might have been fathers who believed in you, or mothers who bolstered your confidence at important times along the journey. As a Brazilian leader whose mother bore over twenty children explained, it might have been a grandmother who saw you and believed God had a call on your life when you might have otherwise gotten lost in the crowd. It might have been a pastor, elder, or layperson who recognized your giftedness and encouraged you to step out of your comfort zone to follow God's leading. It might have been a professor, teacher, youth worker, or countless others who cheered you on and believed in you. I also want to deeply thank each of these people as well.

Most importantly, I want to thank our kind God, who provides us with strength, grace, and opportunities to work with him in mission. What an overwhelming privilege he extends to us! He deserves the ultimate credit and honor if this book yields good fruit in the world.

RESEARCH DETAILS AND
METHODOLOGY

*T*wo overarching questions framed the research that informed what is written in this book: (1) What are diverse women experiencing as they lead in God's mission? (2) What do they believe they need in order to do their best work as leaders in God's mission? While the research is ongoing, currently forty women have been interviewed in person or through video technology. Thirty-four additional women responded to in-depth written surveys. Eight other leaders participated together in three focus groups. And the stories of more than a dozen respected women leaders I have met over the years informed the research as well.

For this reason, the book is based on the journeys of approximately ninety-five women leaders born and raised in the following countries: Australia, Brazil, Burkina Faso, Canada, Chile, Colombia, Ecuador, Egypt, El Salvador, England, Ethiopia, France, Germany, India, Kenya, Korea, Mexico, Netherlands, New Zealand, Nigeria, Norway, Peru, Philippines, Singapore, South Africa, Switzerland, Taiwan, and the United States. Three additional nations will not be mentioned explicitly because of security concerns mission colleagues encounter in those countries.

A purposeful snowball sampling methodology was employed. I started first by contacting women I knew who are deeply respected by their peers, and I then asked them to refer me to other women they knew and respected. I also asked several male leaders to refer me to women leaders they knew and deeply respected. I worked to include diverse types of mission organizations, but I have not mentioned names of organization or churches to lessen risk that people might use that information in harmful ways against them. I also sought to ensure there was cultural, generational, and denominational diversity in the sample.

Someone asked if any Catholics were included in the research. I did not include them because I worked with women I know in a variety of networks, and those tend to be Protestant and evangelical in nature. However, I was deeply affected by my great uncle who was a Franciscan priest. He served in China during World War II caring for orphans, and was taken as a prisoner of war and almost died in an internment camp. A nun I met through my Girl Scout leader when I was young also influenced me greatly. She worked with the poor in Appalachia. My exclusion of Catholic missionaries in the sample is not out of disrespect or disregard for their work; rather, the women included in this study were more accessible through networks where I currently have friends and colleagues serving in mission.

The interview protocols for surveys began with this longer version, which included these questions:

1. Leading as a woman in the mission of God is _____. Please list words or phrases that come to mind and describe why you selected them.

2. What do you find most enjoyable and motivating about leading in God's mission?

3. What do you find most difficult about being a leader? Please describe.

4. Do you think you should lead differently than a man would lead? Why or why not?

5. What does success as a woman leading in mission look like to you?

6. What (if anything) occasionally causes you to feel discouraged, or makes it hard to persevere in your leadership role(s)?

7. What do you need to develop and do your best work as a leader in God's mission?

8. In light of your experiences as a woman leading in mission, how would you answer the following question? (You can be as specific or as general in your answer as you desire. There are no "right" answers, only honest and heartfelt ones. Also, you can wish for multiple things.)

   I wish _____. (Please explain)

9. What advice would you give to young women who are thinking about whether to step into leadership roles in God's mission?

10. What advice would you give to men who want to develop and support women who are called to lead in God's mission?

11. Since leading in God's mission means following him, how have you discerned God's leading? What does "discerning God's leading" look like for you?

12. Are there any additional things you would like to say about this theme of women and leadership in the mission of God?

Once data saturation began occurring in some categories, I switched to a shorter version. This made it easier for people to participate if English was their second, third, or fourth language. Here are the questions employed in that stage:

1. What are the most important leadership lessons you have learned in your journey, and why are these leadership lessons important to you? (Feel free to share stories if you like.)

2. What expectations do people have of women leaders in your cultural and ministry contexts? In what ways are these expectations the same or different than if men were leading in these areas?[1]

3. What do you believe women need to flourish (to fully mature and do their best and most fruitful work) as leaders in God's mission in your culture and ministry context?

4. What have you experienced with regard to your confidence levels at different parts of your leadership journey? (i.e., Have you always felt confident? Have you struggled with a lack of confidence? Have you increased or decreased in confidence over time? Please describe what this has looked like for you.)

Later I deleted question four and added a new question, asking how they sought to live authentically as women leaders in their contexts. I did this because the confidence issue appeared to be tied more to personality type than gender. Each woman asked to complete a survey was also asked to complete an extensive autobiographical questionnaire as well.

I used the individual interviews to explore more about unique issues in women's leadership journeys. Those questions varied based on their backgrounds and experiences. Two questions often asked were, (1) What are the most important lessons you have learned along the journey that shape how you lead in God's mission? (2) Are there things that inspire or discourage you about what you see happening with women leaders in contexts where you have served? (Please explain.)

Each woman participating in the surveys and interviews was asked to sign a consent form and provide explicit additional consent if she wanted her name to be shared when the researcher thought it might benefit others. I opted to use pseudonyms if there seemed to be any chance that mentioning their real names might hinder their ability to get visas in the future, or if there might be unintended risk for others who work with them in God's mission. I also did this to protect the reputation of people who might be mentioned in stories they shared about struggles they faced as a woman in leadership. For three women I used two different pseudonyms to add an extra level of protection in this area.

The most difficult aspect of writing the book was the need to temper academic writing for a popular genre that would be read more extensively, and therefore would be more likely to impact what women experience as they serve and lead in God's mission in the future. In my first draft, I had several quotes under each theme to show thick description and verification that there was data to support each of the ideas and themes I explored. However, my editor coached me to make changes so there were fewer quotes and the text would be easier for different types of readers to absorb. So, if you find yourself wondering if there is thick description, that is indeed the case. However, because this book is written in a popular style, that more extensive level of data could not be included.

Chapter 1: God's Amazing Daughters

[1]Audrey sensed a call from God to work in ministry after raising her children. It was at that time when she began working with an agency in a different part of the world, first in missionary care and later in leadership development.

[2]Before coming to faith in Christ, it was as though God had given me this amazing present that I never chose to open. I guess I was distracted by other things. I knew Jesus was Savior of the world, but I was still trusting that by being a good enough person I would earn my way into heaven some day. And I knew Jesus was Lord of all, but I cared little about what his will was for my life. I basically did what I wanted to do regardless of what he might think about it. If I prayed, it was often like wishing upon a lucky charm rather than approaching a holy and living God. After high school I finally accepted and opened his present. I realized I could be genuinely forgiven for my sins and be in a healed and whole relationship with him that was authentic and lasting through Christ's death, burial, and resurrection. I finally trusted him to be *my* Savior and asked him to be *my* Lord. It was no longer some general understanding, but it was now extremely personal. That is the point when everything changed. A few passages of Scripture that helped me at that time were Romans 5:6-11; 10:8-15; and John 3:16-17.

[3]Carolyn Custis James, *Malestrom: Manhood Swept into the Currents of a Changing World* (Grand Rapids: Zondervan, 2015), 26. Carolyn won a prestigious award for this excellent publication.

[4]I had such a hunger to understand Scripture because I wanted to genuinely know this amazing living God! I also wanted to understand his will for my life. I went back to my Catholic parish, but at that time they did not have Bible studies or ways for people like me to grow in their understanding of God's Word, so I realized I had to look elsewhere.

Because of schooling, work, and ministry I moved frequently, but wherever I lived I was involved in a church. Over the years I have been a part of a Lutheran parish, charismatic churches, a conservative Presbyterian (PCUSA) congregation, a Christian and Missionary Alliance church plant, Willow Creek Community Church (where my husband attended), a Bible church with Southern Baptist roots, a nondenominational church with Christian Reformed roots, and now, after a recent move, an Anglican congregation with strong ties to a Rwandan diocese. I don't think I understood until I wrote this book why God led me in this way. I always thought it was strange because with each move he seemed to lead me to a different type of congregation. But in each place the churches had things in common. Each deeply valued Scripture, and in each place people genuinely loved God and were serious about following Christ as his disciples. What women were allowed to do in each congregation or parish varied significantly, but in each context they found ways to love God and reach out to people who did not know him.

[5]Through my spiritual journey I pray to my heavenly Father in the name of Jesus through the power of the Holy Spirit. I know in many places people alternate male and female pronouns for God because they believe using male pronouns exclusively causes women to be marginalized. I believe Genesis 1:26-27 that both men and women are made in God's image, and I realize that referring to God exclusively with male pronouns might drive some people nuts. But to write differently felt inauthentic to my own spiritual journey and voice. For this reason I ask that you bear with me if this aspect of my writing frustrates you.

[6]Some might wonder why I do not also explore how women were used in God's mission in the Old Testament. The answer is simply space constraints. Since much of that material is available in other forms, I did not include it in this book as well.

[7]John Kirk, *The Mother of the Wesleys: A Biography* (London: Henry James Tresidder, 1986); Charles Wallace Jr., ed., *Susanna Wesley: The Complete Writings* (New York: Oxford University Press, 1997).

[8]"Catherine Booth," *Christianity History* 26 (1990), www.christianitytoday .com/history/people/activists/catherine-booth.html.

[9]Charles Edward Stowe, *The Life of Harriet Beecher Stowe* (New York: Houghton Mifflin, 1889); and "Harriet Beecher Stowe's Life," Harriet Beecher Stowe Center, www.harrietbeecherstowecenter.org/harriet-beecher -stowe/harriet-beecher-stowe-life.

[10]Ruth A. Tucker, *Extraordinary Women of Christian History: What We Can Learn from Their Struggles and Triumphs* (Grand Rapids: Baker, 2016), 130; and "Harriet Tubman," *PBS*, www.pbs.org/wgbh/aia/part4/4p1535.html.

[11]"Frances Jane van Alystyne (Fanny Crosby)," *Faith Hall of Fame*, www.eaec .org/faithhallfame/fanny_crosby.htm.

[12]Janet Benge and Geoff Benge, *Amy Carmichael: Rescuer of Precious Gems*, Christian Heroes Then and Now (Seattle: YWAM Publishing, 1998).

[13]"Lottie Moon Christmas Offering," International Mission Board, www .imb.org/lottie-moon-christmas-offering; "Who Was Lottie Moon?," International Mission Board, www.imb.org/who-was-lottie-moon.

[14]Corrie ten Boom, *The Hiding Place* (New York: Bantam Books, 1974); Halcyon C. Backhouse, *Corrie ten Boom: Faith Triumphs*, Heroes of the Faith (Alton, UK: Hunt & Thorpe, 1992).

[15]Elizabeth Elliott, *Through Gates of Splendor* (New York: Harper, 1957).

[16]Mother Teresa, *No Greater Love* (Novato, CA: New World Library, 1989).

[17]Ruth A. Tucker, "The Role of Bible Women in World Evangelism," *Missiology: An International Review* 13 (1985): 133-46; Paul W. Chilcote and Ulrike Schuler, "Methodist Bible Women in Bulgaria and Italy," *Methodist History* 55 (2017): 108-27; Sunny Hong, "Korean Bible Women on Their Ministry and Social Engagement," American Society of Missiology Annual Meeting, Wheaton, Illinois, 2017.

[18]In her presentation at the American Society of Missiology, Sunny Hong shared that her grandmother was homeless because her grandfather cast her out for not bearing a son. She joined the Korean Bible women and planted seven churches!

[19]Tucker, "Role of Bible Women"; Chilcote and Schuler, "Methodist Bible Women"; Hong, "Korean Bible Women."

[20]Tucker, "Role of Bible Women," 144.

Chapter 2: Navigating Power When Serving

[1]Gladys K. Mwiti, a Kenyan, is a consultant clinical psychologist and psychotrauma specialist with twenty-seven years experience in psychological mental health in Africa and the United States.

[2]Kristen Johnson has been the executive director of two Christian nonprofit organizations, both focused on helping people society often devalues.

[3]Alice H. Eagly and Linda L. Carli address this in their excellent book *Through the Labyrinth: The Truth About How Women Become Leaders* (Boston: Harvard Business School Publishing, 2007). I resonate with the path to leadership they examine; they say it is now less of a glass ceiling than a winding path that often looks quite different for each woman.

[4]Since Leticia is starting a new research position that might require future travel to restricted access countries, her full name will not be shared at this time.

[5]*Power distance* refers to the idea that some parts of Asia societies are more hierarchical in their leadership structures. When this is the case, there often is a significant distance between the primary and the next set of leaders. In more egalitarian cultures, people try to lessen the distance between a leader and others, but in high power distance cultures, people accept that the leader has far greater power. For more on this, see Geert Hofstede and Gert Jan Hofstede, *Cultures and Organizations: Software of the Mind*, 2nd ed. (New York: McGraw-Hill, 2005) 39-72.

[6]Carol Plueddemann has served in a variety of leadership roles over the course of her life and has traveled to approximately fifty nations.

Chapter 3: Being Authentic When Leading

[1]Marie also mentors leaders in a variety of nations and works extensively in the area of board development so mission organizations will have excellent governance to guide ministries.

[2]Sheryl Sandberg, *Lean In: Women, Work, and the Will to Lead* (New York: Random House, 2013).

[3]Deborah Tannen, *Talking from 9 to 5: Women and Men at Work* (New York: HarperCollins, 1994), 161.

[4]Tannen, *Talking from 9 to 5,* 203.

[5]Tannen, *Talking from 9 to 5,* 170.

[6]Tannen, *Talking from 9 to 5,* 164-65.

[7]Tannen, *Talking from 9 to 5,* 202.

[8]Angelika Marsch is deeply respected and served as the executive director for her mission for twelve years. She is now a consultant to other mission leaders in many parts of Europe.

[9]Felecia Thompson is a respected leader in Christian community development.

[10]Donald Atkinson, George Morten, and Derald Wing Sue, *Counseling American Minorities: A Cross-Cultural Perspective*, 2nd ed. (Dubuque, IA: W. C. Brown, 1983).

[11]Havilah Dharamraj led as the Old Testament editor for the *South Asian Bible Commentary*. She has also led in other academic roles and has published a variety of additional resources.

[12]To learn more about this tool, visit "MBTI Basics," Myers & Briggs Foundation, www.myersbriggs.org/my-mbti-personality-type/mbti-basics.

[13]Tannen, *Talking from 9 to 5*, 112.

[14]Herminia Ibarra, Robin J. Ely, and Deborah M. Kolb, "Women Rising: The Unseen Barriers," *Harvard Business Review*, September 2013, 66.

[15]Neide Moura is the executive director of her ministry and has worked in many additional leadership positions.

[16]Ana has worked in leadership in community development initiatives and served as a board member for mission organizations.

Chapter 4: A Distinctive Foundation

[1]Abeni in the past has also led for many years in a restricted-access nation in the area of medical missions.

[2]*Mama Maggie: The Untold Story of One Woman's Mission to Love the Forgotten Children of Egypt's Garbage Slums* (Nashville: Nelson Books, 2015).

[3]The following books capture pieces of the model: Chris Huxham, ed., *Creating Collaborative Advantage* (London: SAGE, 1996); for what this looks like now, visit the Intersector Project website at http://intersector.com; Alan J. Roxburgh and Fred Romanuk, *The Missional Leader: Equipping Your Church to Reach a Changing World* (San Francisco: Jossey-Bass, 2006); George Everly, Douglas Strouse, and George Everly III, *The Secrets of Resilient Leadership: When Failure Is Not an Option . . . Six Essential Characteristics for Leading in Adversity* (New York: Diamedica, 2011); Kwasi Dartey-Baah, "Resilient Leadership: A Transformational-Transactional Leadership Mix," *Journal of Global Responsibility* 6, no. 1 (2015): 99-112; A. H. Eagly, M. C. Johannesen-Schmidt, and M. L. van Engen, "Transformational,

Transactional, and Laissez-Faire Leadership Styles: A Meta-Analysis Comparing Women and Men," *Psychological Bulletin 129*, no. 4(2003): 569-91; Linda Aldoory and Elizabeth Toth, "Leadership and Gender in Public Relations: Perceived Effectiveness of Transformational and Transactional Leadership Styles," *Journal of Public Relations Research* 16, no. 2 (2004): 157-83.

[4]Jim Collins, *Good to Great: Why Some Companies Make the Leap and Others Don't* (New York: Harper Business, 2001). Jim Collins has a short video that captures this aspect of Level 5 leaders on his website: www.jimcollins.com/concepts/level-five-leadership.html.

[5]See "Start Here: What Is Servant Leadership?," Center for Servant Leadership, www.greenleaf.org/what-is-servant-leadership; or Robert K. Greenleaf, "Servant Leadership," www.american.edu/spa/leadership/application/upload/Greenleaf,%20Servant%20Leadership.pdf.

[6]Ellen Livingood is a respected leader in church mission mobilization.

[7]Themes raised by these women mirror a number of concepts mentioned in the first chapter of Rick Warren's book *The Purpose Driven Life* (Grand Rapids: Zondervan, 2002), 22-29. However the women never mentioned this book as being the focal point for why they believed this way. While it is likely that some read the book in prior years, the overall sense was this starting point is a sign of genuine discipleship where Christ is Lord rather than self-centered or in-group-centered ambitions being the foundation or driving force. If this is a new concept for you, a friend of mine published a book in North America that might be of interest. See Sharon Hodde Miller, *Free of Me: Why Life Is Better When It's Not About You* (Grand Rapids: Baker, 2017).

[8]Carmen Castillo Felber has held national and area leadership roles on her continent and also preaches in her local congregation.

Chapter 5: Connected in Different Ways

[1]Angelika Marsch explains her perception of how women lead in light of her extensive leadership experience in Bible translation ministries.

[2]Robert J. House, Paul J. Hanges, Mansour Javidan, Peter W. Dorfman, and Vipin Gupta, eds., *Culture, Leadership, and Organizations: The GLOBE Study of 62 Societies* (Thousand Oaks, CA: SAGE, 2004).

[3]Geert Hofstede and Gert Jan Hofstede, *Cultures and Organizations: Software of the Mind*, 2nd ed. (New York: McGraw-Hill, 2005).

[4]Karen Swanson leads in correctional ministries by supporting and equipping others who minister in jails and prisons and by assisting with reentry and rehabilitation efforts of incarcerated individuals.

[5]Jenny Collins is one of the people who developed the "Standards of Excellence in Short-Term Mission" for the United States.

[6]For a fuller understanding of the impact of and reactions to the social gospel, see A. Russell, "The Social Gospel," in the *Global Dictionary of Theology*, ed. William A. Dyrness and Veli-Matti Kärkkäinen (Downers Grove, IL: IVP Academic, 2008), 837-39.

[7]Jawanza Kunjufu, *Countering the Conspiracy to Destroy Black Boys* (Chicago: African American Images, 2004), 31-55.

[8]The woman who shared this comment and who I quoted a few other times in this book, is an exceptional leader, interculturalist, academic, and professional in her field. The complexity in the research is frustrating because I would love to cite her work, but I'm concerned it might have bad ripple effects for others if I do.

Chapter 6: Persevering with Wisdom

[1]Sanuja is single and cares for her mother in the midst of her leadership responsibilities. Her mission advocates on behalf of marginalized communities seeking to eliminate catastrophic diseases.

[2]See Jack Mezirow, *Transformative Dimensions of Adult Learning* (San Francisco: Jossey-Bass, 1991); and Patricia Cranton, *Understanding and Promoting Transformative Learning* (Sterling, VA: Stylus, 2016).

[3]Miroslav Volf, *Exclusion and Embrace* (Nashville: Abingdon, 1996), 126.

[4]Cornelius Plantinga, *Not the Way It's Supposed to Be: A Breviary of Sin* (Grand Rapids: Eerdmans, 1996).

Chapter 7: Prioritizing Impact and Excellence

[1]Yvonne has led in a variety of ministry contexts such as large mission agencies, emerging entrepreneurial startups, with young adults in higher education, and also in congregations.

[2]Joyce Rees was the director of a ministry that serves some of the most hurting people in her nation. She also serves as a pastor and trains teams of lay preachers.

Chapter 8: Caring About Challenges

[1]Hannah explains the challenge of fitting in when she does not fit the stereotypical mold. She has led diverse teams and overseen global communication and strategy, helping her mission to find new and creative ways to overcome structural barriers to work in greater collaboration and fruitfulness with the global church.

Chapter 9: Strategies That Accommodate Others

[1]Alima works alongside other teams that focus on Bible translation, so her work in literacy enables people to understand Scripture. Literacy is a social justice issue, for it is tied to growing levels of economic well-being, better health outcomes for children, and so forth. She has also served in a variety of additional leadership positions, such as the executive director of her mission in times of leadership transition.

[2]I have exercised additional care to disguise the identities of the women in this section of the book.

Chapter 10: When Accommodation Hinders Faithfulness

[1]Semira leads in compassion ministries for children, and she mentors emerging leaders in her own nation and in other parts of the world.

Chapter 11: If Married, Husbands Who Act Like Jesus

[1]This quote is from my journey. I never realized my husband had made this vow to God until more than a decade into our marriage. He had always been so supportive of my ministry, even when it meant he would be inconvenienced by my travel and schedule. His words still encourage me when I encounter intense seasons of ministry.

[2]I think it is equally inappropriate and dishonoring to God when women verbally malign their husbands in private or in public.

[3]Marty Makary and Ellen Vaughn, *Mama Maggie: The Untold Story of One Woman's Mission to Love the Forgotten Children of Egypt's Garbage Slums* (Nashville: Nelson Books, 2015), 55.

Chapter 12: A Healthier Metaphor in the Workplace

[1]Melissa has served as a missionary in underresourced communities in Africa and within her own nation.

[2]Mary Lederleitner, *Cross-Cultural Partnerships: Navigating the Complexities of Money and Mission* (Downers Grove, IL: InterVarsity Press, 2010).

[3]William M. Struthers, *Wired for Intimacy: How Pornography Hijacks the Male Brain* (Downers Grove, IL: InterVarsity Press, 2010).

[4]Sue Edwards, Kelley Matthews, and Henry J. Rogers, *Mixed Ministry: Working Together as Brothers and Sisters in an Oversexed Society* (Grand Rapids: Kregel Academic, 2008), 231-37. The epilogue is titled "New Beginnings for Sacred Siblings."

Chapter 13: Men Courageously Opening Opportunities

[1]Natalia has served alongside her husband for decades starting new campus ministries and ministries for families.

[2]Wendy Wilson is the executive director of a ministry that focuses on developing women leaders, and she is a women's leadership consultant for one of the most respected mission networks in North America.

Chapter 14: Cultivating Encouragement and Growth

[1]Lisa Anderson-Umana has also completed a dissertation on leadership emergence, growth, and culture among evangelical pastors in Tegucigalpa, Honduras.

[2]Deborah Tannen, *Talking from 9 to 5: Women and Men at Work* (New York: HarperCollins, 1994).

[3]Sharon Daloz Parks, *Big Questions, Worthy Dreams: Mentoring Young Adults in Their Search for Meaning, Purpose, and Faith*, 10th anniv. ed. (San Francisco: Jossey-Bass, 2011).

[4]Parks, *Big Questions*, 174.

[5]Parks, *Big Questions*, 174.

[6]Parks, *Big Questions*, 176.

[7]Parks, *Big Questions*, 176.

[8]Parks, *Big Questions*, 176-96.

[9]Parks, *Big Questions*, 185.

[10]Parks, *Big Questions*, 190-97.

[11]I really like this article for women written by Deborah Gin, "Complete Your Crew: Mentoring and More," Association of Theological Schools, accessed July 31, 2017, www.ats.edu/search/google/complete%20your%20crew.

Chapter 15: Addressing Remaining Issues

[1]Nicole at times travels extensively to help leaders and organizations involved in Bible translation, literacy, and community development grow to their full potential.

[2]Carol Plueddemann shared this insight as we talked, and I thought it was quite insightful and helpful for women who are in seasons of transition that cause them to feel that their opportunities for growth are stunted.

[3]I would like to share a caveat that I believe is also important. I don't mean to infer that women have no responsibility in this type of discussion. It is essential for women not to expect male colleagues to provide them with the same level of empathy and understanding that women colleagues have provided over the years. Women also bear the responsibility of discerning and reading their work context, and they often need to adapt the scope and intensity of what they share in light of what is appropriate both culturally and in a mixed-gender workplace. Additionally, women bear responsibility to monitor the impact of how they communicate with others about health issues they are facing.

[4]See the excellent article by Wendy Wilson, "Negotiating the No," *Mission CEO Survey Report*, Stone Mountain, GA, 2016.

[5]Amy B. Diehl and Leanne M. Dzubinski. "Making the Invisible Visible: A Cross-Sector Analysis of Gender-Based Leadership Barriers," *Human Resource Development Quarterly* 27, no. 2 (2016): 181-206.

Conclusion

[1]Carolyn Custis James, *Lost Women of the Bible: The Women We Thought We Knew* (Grand Rapids: Zondervan, 2005), 16.

[2]Michelle Lee-Barnewall, *Neither Complementarian nor Egalitarian: A Kingdom Corrective to the Evangelical Gender Debate* (Grand Rapids: Baker Academic, 2017).

[3]Mama Maggie, quoted in Marty Makary and Ellen Vaughn, *Mama Maggie: The Untold Story of One Woman's Mission to Love the Forgotten Children of Egypt's Garbage Slums* (Nashville: Nelson Books, 2015), 11.

[4]Carolyn Custis James, *Malestrom: Manhood Swept into the Currents of a Changing World* (Grand Rapids: Zondervan, 2015), 26.

Acknowledgments

[1]Sadly, a great deal of religious persecution happens around the world. It ranges from denied visas to physical harm to a person, family members, and colleagues. To learn more about what many Christians are facing around the world, see the Templeton study *Under Caesar's Sword: Christian Response to Persecution* (Notre Dame, IN: University of Notre Dame's Center for Ethics and Culture, 2017) or stories from the Voice of the Martyrs book *Hearts of Fire: Eight Women in the Underground Church and Their Stories of Costly Faith* (Bartlesville, OK: VOM Books, 2015).

Appendix

[1]I asked this question, and questions four and five in the long version of the survey, as a way to tease out gender differences. I sometimes asked similar questions in the face-to-face and video interviews. We know from the GLOBE research that different cultures and nations have differing opinions about what comprises "good leadership." See Robert J. House, Paul J. Hanges, Mansour Javidan, Peter W. Dorfman, and Vipin Gupta, eds., *Culture, Leadership, and Organizations: The GLOBE Study of 62 Societies* (Thousand Oaks, CA: SAGE, 2004). However, I wanted to see what impact being female had on their leadership styles and preferences. This strategy proved to be effective.

BIBLIOGRAPHY

Adler, Nancy J. "Global Leadership: Women Leaders." *Management International Review* 37, no. 1 (1997): 171-96.

Atkinson, Donald R., George Morten, and Derald Wing Sue. *Counseling American Minorities: A Cross-Cultural Perspective.* 2nd ed. Dubuque, IA: W. C. Brown, 1983.

Backhouse, Halcyon C. *Corrie ten Boom: Faith Triumphs.* Heroes of the Faith. Alton, UK: Hunt & Thorpe, 1992.

Bancroft, Barbara. *Running on Empty: The Gospel for Women in Ministry.* Greensboro, NC: New Growth Press, 2014.

Barton, Ruth Haley. *Life Together in Christ: Experiencing Transformation in Community.* Downers Grove, IL: InterVarsity Press, 2014.

———. *Pursuing God's Will Together: A Discernment Practice for Leadership Groups.* Downers Grove, IL: InterVarsity Press, 2012.

———. *Strengthening the Soul of Your Leadership: Seeking God in the Crucible of Ministry.* Downers Grove, IL: InterVarsity Press, 2008.

Benge, Janet, and Geoff Benge. *Amy Carmichael: Rescuer of Precious Gems.* Christian Heroes Then and Now. Seattle: YWAM Publishing, 1998.

Bohm, David. *On Dialogue.* New York: Routledge, 1996.

Boom, Corrie ten. *The Hiding Place.* New York: Bantam Books, 1974.

Calhoun, Adele Ahlberg. *Spiritual Disciplines Handbook: Practices That Transform Us.* Downers Grove, IL: InterVarsity Press, 2005.

"Catherine Booth." *Christianity History* 26 (1990). www.christianitytoday.com/history/people/activists/catherine-booth.html.

Chilcote, Paul W., and Ulrike Schuler. "Methodist Bible Women in Bulgaria and Italy." *Methodist History* 55 (2017): 108-27.

Choi, Hyaeweol. *Gender and Mission Encounters in Korea: New Women, Old Ways.* Berkeley: University of California Press, 2009.

Collins, Jim. *Good to Great: Why Some Companies Make the Leap and Others Don't.* New York: Harper Business, 2001.

———. "Level 5 Leadership." *Jim Collins.* www.jimcollins.com/concepts /level-five-leadership.html.

Corbin, Juliet, and Anselm Strauss. *Basics of Qualitative Research.* 3rd ed. Thousand Oaks, CA: Sage, 2008.

Cranton, Patricia. *Understanding and Promoting Transformative Learning.* Sterling, VA: Stylus, 2016.

Dharmaraj, Glory E. "Women as Border-Crossing Agents: Transforming the Center from the Margins." *Missiology* 26, no. 1 (1998): 55-66.

Diehl, Amy B., and Leanne M. Dzubinski. "Making the Invisible Visible: A Cross-Sector Analysis of Gender-Based Leadership Barriers." *Human Resource Development Quarterly* 27, no. 2 (2016): 181-206.

Downes, Donna. "Confused Missionary Roles—Theirs or Mine?" In *Frontline Women: Negotiating Crosscultural Issues in Ministry.* Edited by Marguerite G. Kraft. Pasadena, CA: William Carey Library, 2003, 101-22.

Dzubinski, Leanne M. "Playing by the Rules: How Women Lead in Evangelical Organizations." PhD diss., University of Georgia, 2013.

———. "Portrayal vs. Practice: Contemporary Women's Contribution to Christian Mission." *Missiology: An International Review* 44, no. 1 (2016): 78-94.

Eagly, Alice H., and Linda L. Carli. *Through the Labyrinth: The Truth About How Women Become Leaders.* Boston: Harvard Business School Press, 2007.

Eagly, A. H., M. C. Johannesen-Schmidt, and M. L. van Engen. "Transformational, Transactional, and Laissez-Faire Leadership Styles: A Meta-Analysis Comparing Women and Men." *Psychological Bulletin* 129, no. 4 (2003): 569-91.

Edwards, Sue, Kelley Matthews, and Henry J. Rogers. *Mixed Ministry: Working Together as Brothers and Sisters in an Oversexed Society.* Grand Rapids: Kregel Academic & Professional, 2008.

Elliott, Elisabeth. *Through Gates of Splendor.* New York: Harper, 1957.

Everly, George Jr., Douglas Strouse, and George Everly III. *The Secrets of Resilient Leadership: When Failure Is Not an Option . . . Six Essential Characteristics for Leading in Adversity.* New York: Diamedica, 2011.

"Frances Jane van Alystyne (Fanny Crosby)." *Faith Hall of Fame.* www .eaec.org/faithhallfame/fanny_crosby.htm.

Gin, Deborah. "Complete Your Crew: Mentoring and More." Association of Theological Schools. Accessed July 31, 2017. www.ats.edu/uploads /resources/publications-presentations/documents/complete-your-crew .pdf.

Griffiths, Valeria. *Not Less Than Everything: The Courageous Women Who Carried the Christian Gospel to China.* Oxford: Monarch Books, 2004.

"Harriet Beecher Stowe's Life." Harriet Beecher Stowe Center. www.harriet beecherstowecenter.org/harriet-beecher-stowe/harriet-beecher-stowe -life.

"Harriet Tubman." PBS. www.pbs.org/wgbh/aia/part4/4p1535.html.

Hiebert, Frances. "Why We've Missed the Mark." *Christian Leader* 26 (April 1988).

Hofstede, Geert, and Gert Hofstede. *Cultures and Organizations: Software of the Mind.* 2nd ed. New York: McGraw-Hill, 2005.

Hong, Sunny. "Korean Bible Women on Their Ministry and Social Engagement." American Society of Missiology Annual Meeting, 2017.

House, Robert J., Paul J. Hanges, Mansour Javidan, Peter W. Dorfman, and Vipin Gupta, eds. *Culture, Leadership, and Organizations: The GLOBE Study of 62 Societies.* Thousand Oaks, CA: SAGE, 2004.

Huxham, Chris, ed. *Creating Collaborative Advantage.* London: Sage, 1996.

Ibarra, Herminia, Robin Ely, and Deborah Kolb. "Women Rising: The Unseen Barriers." *Harvard Business Review,* September 2013, 60-66.

Intersector Project. http://intersector.com.

Isaacs, William. *Dialogue and the Art of Thinking Together.* New York: Doubleday, 1999.

James, Carolyn Custis. *Lost Women of the Bible: The Women We Thought We Knew*. Grand Rapids: Zondervan, 2005.

———. *Malestrom: Manhood Swept into the Currents of a Changing World*. Grand Rapids: Zondervan, 2015.

Johnson, Alan F., ed. *How I Changed My Mind About Women in Leadership*. Grand Rapids: Zondervan, 2010.

Kennedy, Jessica A., and Laura J. Kray. "Who Is Willing to Jeopardize Ethical Values for Money and Social Status? Gender Differences in Reactions to Ethical Compromises." *Social Psychology & Personality Science* 5, no. 1 (2014): 52-59.

King, Jeanne Porter, and Gabriella M. Lindsay. *That's What She Said! 366 Leadership Quotes by Women*. South Holland, IL: TransPorter Group, 2017.

Kirk, John. *The Mother of the Wesleys: A Biography*. London: Henry James Tresidder, 1986.

Kraft, Marguerite G., ed. *Frontline Women: Negotiating Cross-Cultural Issues in Ministry*. Pasadena, CA: William Carey Library, 2003.

Kunjufu, Jawanza. "Fourth Grade Failure Syndrome." *In Countering the Conspiracy to Destroy Black Boys*. Chicago: African American Images, 2004.

Kwasi, Dartey-Baah. "Resilient Leadership: A Transformational-Transactional Leadership Mix." *Journal of Global Responsibility* 6, no. 1 (2015): 99-112.

Lederleitner, Mary. *Cross-Cultural Partnerships: Navigating the Complexities of Money and Mission*. Downers Grove, IL: InterVarsity Press, 2010.

———. "Leading Authentically as a Woman—Plenary Session." Wycliffe Global Alliance. Kusadasi, Turkey, 2015.

Lee-Barnewall, Michelle. *Neither Complementarian nor Egalitarian: A Kingdom Corrective to the Evangelical Gender Debate*. Grand Rapids: Baker Academic, 2017.

"Lottie Moon Christmas Offering." International Mission Board. www.imb.org/lottie-moon-christmas-offering.

Loumagne, Jenna. "Biola Professor Present Research on Unconscious Gender Bias in the Workplace." *Biola News*, July 19, 2017. http://now

.biola.edu/news/article/2017/jul/19/biola-professor-presents -research-unconscious-gend.

Makary, Marty, and Ellen Vaughn. *Mama Maggie: The Untold Story of One Woman's Mission to Love the Forgotten Children of Egypt's Garbage Slums.* Nashville: Nelson Books, 2015.

Marsch, Angelika, and Martina Kessler. "Women Lead Differently." *Personal Perspectives,* 2-14.

Merriam, Sharan B. *Qualitative Research: A Guide to Design and Implementation.* San Francisco: Jossey-Bass, 2009.

Mezirow, Jack. *Transformative Dimensions of Adult Learning.* San Francisco: Jossey-Bass, 1991

Mother Teresa. *No Greater Love.* Novato, CA: New World Library, 1989.

Park, Bokyoung. "A Hidden Figure of Korean Mission History: Life and Ministry of Kwang-Myung Kim." American Society of Missiology Annual Meeting, Wheaton, IL, 2017.

Parks, Sharon Daloz. *Big Questions, Worthy Dreams: Mentoring Young Adults in Their Search for Meaning, Purpose, and Faith.* 10th anniv. ed. San Francisco: Jossey-Bass, 2011.

Patton, Michael Quinn. *Qualitative Research & Evaluation Methods.* 3rd ed. Thousand Oaks, CA: Sage, 2002.

Plantinga, Cornelius. *Not the Way It's Supposed to Be: A Breviary of Sin.* Grand Rapids: Eerdmans, 1996.

Rhode, Deborah L. *Women and Leadership.* New York: Oxford University Press, 2017.

Roxburgh, Alan J., and Fred Romanuk. *The Missional Leader: Equipping Your Church to Reach a Changing World.* San Francisco: Jossey-Bass, 2006.

Russell, A. "The Social Gospel." In *Global Dictionary of Theology.* Edited by William A. Dyrness and Veli-Matti Kärkkäinen. Downers Grove, IL: IVP Academic, 2008.

Sandberg, Sheryl. *Lean In: Women, Work and the Will to Lead.* New York: Random House, 2013.

Schein, Edgar. *Humble Inquiry: The Gentle Art of Asking Instead of Telling.* San Francisco: Berrett-Koelher, 2013.

"Start Here: What Is Servant Leadership?" Center for Servant Leadership. www.greenleaf.org/what-is-servant-leadership.

Storberg-Walker, Julia, and Paige Haber-Curran, eds. *Theorizing Women and Leadership: New Insights and Contributions from Multiple Perspectives.* International Leadership Association Series. Charlotte, NC: IAP, 2017.

Stowe, Charles Edward. *The Life of Harriet Beecher Stowe.* New York: Houghton Mifflin, 1889.

Struthers, William M. *Wired for Intimacy: How Pornography Highjacks the Male Brain.* Downers Grove, IL: InterVarsity Press, 2010.

Tannen, Deborah, ed. *Gender and Conversation Interaction.* Oxford Studies in Sociolinguistics. New York: Oxford University Press, 1993.

————*Talking from 9 to 5: Women and Men at Work.* New York: HarperCollins, 1994.

Templeton Religious Trust. *Under Caesar's Sword: Christian Response to Persecution.* Notre Dame, IN: Center for Ethics and Culture, 2017.

Tong, Joy K. C., and Fenggang Yang. "The Femininity of Chinese Christianity: A Chinese Charismatic Church and Its Female Leadership." *Review of Religion and Chinese Society* 1, no. 2 (2014): 195-211.

Tucker, Ruth A. *Extraordinary Women of Christian History: What We Can Learn from Their Struggles and Triumphs.* Grand Rapids: Baker, 2016.

————. "The Role of Bible Women in World Evangelism." *Missiology: An International Review* 13 (1985): 133-146.

Voice of the Martyrs. *Hearts of Fire: Eight Women in the Underground Church and Their Stories of Costly Faith.* Bartlesville, OK: VOM Books, 2015.

Volf, Miroslav. *Exclusion & Embrace.* Nashville: Abingdon Press, 1996.

Wallace, Charles, Jr., ed. *Susanna Wesley: The Complete Writings.* New York: Oxford University Press, 1997.

Warren, Rick. *The Purpose Driven Life.* Grand Rapids: Zondervan, 2002.

Weng Kit, Cheong. "The (dis)Empowerment of Pentecostal-Charismatic Chinese Women in Malaysia and Singapore." Kota Kinabalu, Malaysia: Sabah Theological Seminary.

"Who Was Lottie Moon?" International Mission Board. www.imb.org/who-was-lottie-moon.

Wilson, Wendy. "Negotiating the No." *Mission CEO Survey Report.* Stone Mountain, GA, 2016.

Wintle, Brian, Havilah Dharamraj, Jesudason Baskar Jeyaraj, Paul Swarup, Jacob Cherian, and Finny Philip, eds. *South Asian Bible Commentary.* Cumbria, UK: Langham Partnership, 2015.

Wright, Christopher J. H. *The Mission of God: Unlocking the Bible's Grand Narrative.* Downers Grove, IL: IVP Academic, 2006.

Warner, Shawna, Leanne M. Dzubinski, Sarah Wood, and Colleen Marti. "Justice Meets Justification: Women's Need for Holistic Ministry in World Mission." *Missiology: An International Review* 45, no. 1 (2017): 67-87.

"Women's Commission." World Evangelical Alliance. www.world evangelicals.org/wc.

ABOUT THE AUTHOR

*M*ary T. Lederleitner has held a variety of mission leadership roles. From 1997 to 2017 she served with Wycliffe and traveled extensively to many nations. The first decade was spent in a variety of financial leadership roles while the next decade was spent in thought-leadership positions as a researcher, author, conference speaker, and missiologist. During the last eight years with Wycliffe, Mary served as a consultant on the executive team of the Wycliffe Global Alliance.

Because her areas of research kept expanding, she transitioned out of Wycliffe and in 2018 founded Missional Intelligence, a new ministry that works under the auspices of Faith & Learning International. She is the executive director, working with leaders to find answers to diverse challenges that are hindering the effectiveness of their ministries.

Mary has an MA in intercultural studies from Wheaton College and a PhD in educational studies from Trinity Evangelical Divinity School, and she serves as an adjunct professor in the graduate programs of both of these academic institutions. She is author of the book *Cross-Cultural Partnerships: Navigating the Complexities of Money and Mission*. She also completed a dissertation examining the experiences of twenty-somethings, specifically what was helping and hindering them from finding their places in faith communities after graduation from university. She has contributed chapters and academic articles to a variety of books and journals.

Mary serves on the boards of Catalyst Services and OM Global. She also serves on the Wheaton College Board of Visitors and as a Billy Graham Evangelism Fellow. She is from a large family with four brothers, two sisters, and lots of nieces and nephews. In her late thirties she met and married her husband, John. They enjoy going through life together and watching God's surprises unfold as they seek to follow Christ's leading. She can be reached through email at MaryL@missional-intelligence.net.